Oliver P. (Oliver Perry) Shiras

Equity Practice in the United States Circuit Courts

A Compilation of the Provisions Governing the Same as Found....

Oliver P. (Oliver Perry) Shiras

Equity Practice in the United States Circuit Courts
A Compilation of the Provisions Governing the Same as Found....

ISBN/EAN: 9783337159153

Printed in Europe, USA, Canada, Australia, Japan

Cover: Foto ©Suzi / pixelio.de

More available books at **www.hansebooks.com**

EQUITY PRACTICE

IN THE

UNITED STATES CIRCUIT COURTS.

A COMPILATION

OF THE

PROVISIONS GOVERNING THE SAME AS FOUND IN
THE STATUTES OF THE UNITED STATES,
RULES IN EQUITY AND DECISIONS
OF THE SUPREME COURT.

BY

OLIVER P. SHIRAS,

DISTRICT JUDGE FOR THE NORTHERN
DISTRICT OF IOWA.

SECOND EDITION.

REVISED AND ENLARGED.

CHICAGO:
CALLAGHAN AND COMPANY.
1898.

The creation of the Circuit Courts of Appeal and the radical change caused thereby in the matter of appeals is the justification for the issuance of a second edition of the following manual.

Though revised and somewhat enlarged, the purpose of this, as of the first edition, is not to present a treatise on equity jurisdiction and practice at large, but only to bring together in compact form the provisions found in the Rules in Equity, in the Statutes of the United States and in the decisions of the Supreme Court, which define and limit Federal jurisdiction in equity and which prescribe and explain the steps required to be taken in bringing, preparing for hearing and submitting suits in equity, in taking appeals therein, and in enforcing decrees by direct or auxiliary process and proceedings.

DUBUQUE, IOWA, 1897.

METHOD OF PROCEDURE

IN

EQUITY CAUSES

IN

THE UNITED STATES CIRCUIT COURTS.

CHAPTER I.

THE CIRCUIT COURT AS A COURT OF EQUITY — JURISDICTION — RULE DAYS — MOTIONS AND ORDERS GRANTABLE BY CLERK OR JUDGE.

I. With the exception of cases to which a state is a party, or which affect ambassadors, foreign ministers, their domestic servants, consuls or vice-consuls, of which, by section 2, article 3, of the constitution and section 687 of the Revised Statutes, original jurisdiction is conferred upon the supreme court, and of cases arising under the revenue, national banking and bankrupt laws, and the few other special matters enumerated in section 563 of the Revised Statutes, in which jurisdiction, exclusive or concurrent, is conferred upon the district courts, the original jurisdiction of causes in equity, cognizable in the courts of the United States, is vested in the circuit courts.

Revised Statutes, section 629; 18 Statutes at Large, 470; 25 Statutes at Large, 433.

II. The forms of process used and the modes of procedure had in suits in equity in the courts of the United States are according to the principles, rules and usages obtaining in courts of equitable jurisdiction, and especially in the high court of chancery in England, subject to alteration or addition by statute or by rules of courts duly adopted; power being given to the supreme court to adopt from time to time general rules for the regulation of the equity practice in all the courts of the United States, under which authority a series of rules have been promulgated, known as *The Rules of Practice for the Courts of Equity of the United States.*

Revised Statutes, sections 913, 917. Rule 90.

III. The circuit courts, as courts of equity, are always open for the purpose of filing bills, answers and other pleadings, for the issuance of process and for the making all interlocutory motions, orders and rules, and the directing such other proceedings as may be necessary to prepare causes for hearing upon their merits.

Rule 1.

IV. The first Monday of each month is a rule day, on which days the clerk is required to be in attendance at his office for the purpose of receiving, entering and disposing of all motions, rules, orders and other proceedings grantable as a matter of course.

Rule 2.

V. All motions and applications filed in the clerk's office, for the issuing of subpœnas for defendants, subpœnas for witnesses, for filing bills, answers, exceptions, pleas, demurrers and other pleadings; for making amendments to bills before answer, plea or demurrer thereto; for making amendments to answers before replication thereto; for taking bills *pro confesso* for want of entry of appearance, or for want of a pleading; for filing exceptions and all other proceedings which do not require action by the court or judge thereon, are deemed matters grantable of course.

Upon cause shown, proceedings had as matter of course may be altered, suspended or rescinded by a judge of the court.

Rule 5.

VI. Either of the judges of the court may at any time at chambers, or on the rule days at the clerk's office, make and direct all such interlocutory orders, rules and other proceedings as may be needed to prepare causes for hearing upon their merits.

This rule is intended to apply to such proceedings as are not grantable as a matter of course by the clerk, but which require the action of the court or a judge thereon.

In some instances the order, leave or rule may be granted by the court or judge without notice to the adversary party of such application.

In others, notice must be given.

Where the rules provide that notice shall be given of an application for a certain order or other proceeding, such notice is essential,— and unless a different time is assigned by a judge, the same will be for hearing on the rule day next after that on which the motion is made.

Where the rules provide that a court or judge may grant a named order or leave, but is silent in regard to notice, then the same may be granted without notice other than the entry upon the order book by the clerk, although the court or judge may, at discretion, require notice to be given.

Application for orders, rules and other proceedings may be made orally or in writing.

Generally, the better practice is to prepare the application in writing and submit or send it to the judge, asking him to indorse the required order or leave thereon, or, if notice is required of the application, to indorse thereon the time and place of hearing the same, of which notice must be given to the adversary party or his solicitor.

Rule 6.

VII. It is the duty of the clerk to keep an order book, in which is entered, on the day they are made, all motions, rules, orders and other proceedings made and directed at chambers or on the rule days, and, except in cases where personal or other notice is specially required or directed, the entry in such order book is notice to the parties and their solicitors of such motion, order, rule or other proceeding.

Rule 4.

CHAPTER II.

FEDERAL JURISDICTION IN EQUITY.

VIII. The jurisdiction of the circuit courts of the United States, as courts of equity, is subject to two general limitations, and before bringing suit therein careful consideration should be given to the two questions: is the case such, with respect to the rights sought to be enforced or protected or with respect to the remedy desired, that it comes within the recognized boundaries of jurisdiction in equity, as distinguished from jurisdiction at law, and if so, is the case one which, by reason of the subject-matter or by reason of the diverse citizenship or citizenship and alienage of the adversary parties, comes within federal cognizance as the same is created and defined in the statutes of the United States.

A discussion or statement in detail of the grounds, extent and limitations of jurisdiction in equity is not within the scope of this manual, and therefore all that will be said with respect thereto is that the sources of federal equitable jurisdiction will be found in the principles established by the high court of chancery in England and recognized by the courts of the United States as applicable to the existing conditions in the United States,[1] in the acts of congress conferring jurisdiction in equity in special matters, and in the acts of state legislatures creating new rights properly enforceable in equity, according to the rules governing that practice in the federal courts.[2]

[1] Robinson v. Campbell, 3 Wheat., 222; State of Pennsylvania v. Bridge Co., 13 How., 518; Kirby v. Lake Shore, etc., R. R. Co., 120 U. S., 130; Mississippi Mills v. Cohn, 150 U. S., 202; Bardon v. Land, etc., Co., 157 U. S., 327.

[2] Clark v. Smith, 13 Peters, 195; Broderick's Will Case, 21 Wall., 503; Holland v. Challen, 110 U. S., 15; Reynolds v. Bank, 112 U. S., 405; Frost v. Spitley, 121 U. S., 552; Ridings v. Johnson, 128 U. S., 212; Cowley v. Northern Pacific R. R. Co., 159 U. S., 569.

IX. In section 723 of the Revised Statutes, reenacting section 16 of the judiciary act of 1789, it is provided that "suits in equity shall not be sustained in either of the courts of the United States in any case where a plain, adequate and complete remedy may be had at law." Under the provisions of this section and those of the seventh amendment to the constitution declaring that in suits at common law, when the value in controversy exceeds $20, the right of trial by jury shall be preserved, it is held that to sustain the right to proceed in the circuit court as a court of equity, it must appear in the given cause that from the nature of the controversy, or of the relief sought, a plain, adequate and complete remedy at law does not exist, according to the remedies at law in existence when the act of 1789 was adopted or such as may have been since provided by act of congress.

Dade v. Irwin, 2 How., 383; Parker v. Winnipisiogee Co., 2 Black, 545; Watson v. Sutherland, 5 Wall., 74; Barber v. Barber, 21 How., 582; Thompson v. Railroad Co., 6 Wall., 134; Hayward v. Andrews, 106 U. S., 672; N. Y. Co. v. Memphis Water Co., 107 U. S., 485; Litchfield v. Ballou, 114 U. S., 190; Thompson v. Allen Co., 115 U. S., 550; Buzard v. Houston, 119 U. S., 347; McConihay v. Wright, 121 U. S., 201; Whitehead v. Shattuck, 138 U. S., 146; Waterman v. McKenzie, 138 U. S., 252; Scott v. Neely, 140 U. S., 105; Lacassagne v. Chapuis, 144 U. S., 119.

X. If the case contains some one or more of the recognized grounds of jurisdiction in equity, the remedy at law, if one exists, to exclude jurisdiction in equity must be as practical, as complete, as prompt and as efficient, not only with respect to the immediate action, but in obviating the need for further litigation concerning the subject-matter of the controversy, and in preventing irreparable or continuing injury and damage.

Boyce's Executors v. Grundy, 3 Peters, 210; Parker v. Company, 2 Black, 545; Insurance Co. v. Bailey, 3 Peters, 210; Kilbourn v. Sunderland, 130 U. S., 505; Joy v. St. Louis, 138 U. S., 1; Tyler v. Savage, 143 U. S., 79; D. M. Osborne & Co. v. Mo. Pacific Ry. Co., 147 U. S., 248.

XI. If the case is one within jurisdiction in equity, then consideration must be given to the question whether the controversy is such that a circuit court of the United States can take jurisdiction over the same, or, in other words, is the case one of federal cognizance.

The jurisdiction of the courts of the United States cannot be extended, by congressional action, beyond the limitations fixed by the provisions of the constitution, as contained in articles III and XI thereof, and the jurisdiction of the circuit courts, being courts not named in the constitution, but created by act of congress, is such and such only as is expressly conferred thereby.

Under the provisions of the constitution, congress can confer upon the circuit courts jurisdiction over all cases arising under the constitution, laws or treaties of the United States, over controversies to which the United States is a party, or which are between citizens of different states, or between citizens of the same state claiming lands under grants from different states, or between a citizen of a state of the Union and foreign states, citizens or subjects.

The circuit courts were created by the original judiciary act of 1789 and its provisions, with the amendments thereto, re-enacted in 1873, as title XIII of the Revised Statutes, and the amendatory acts of 1875 and 1888 contain the provisions now in force, creating and defining the general jurisdiction of the circuit courts.

XII. As the terms of the act of 1888, as well as those in the preceding acts of which it is amendatory, with respect to the jurisdiction of the circuit courts, are limited to those cases wherein jurisdiction exists concurrently in the federal and state courts, its provisions in this respect are not applicable to cases over which the federal jurisdiction is exclusive, and touching which there are special grants of jurisdiction to be found in the statutes of the United States, such as cases arising under any act for providing for revenue from imports[1] or tonnage[1] or from internal taxes,[1] or arising under the acts authorizing the issuance of patents and forbidding the infringement thereof,[2] or under the acts regulating copyrights,[3] or under the provisions of the national bank act for the purpose of winding up the affairs of a national bank,[4] or under the interstate commerce acts,[5] or under the acts prohibiting trusts in matters connected with interstate and foreign commerce,[6] or under the act providing for a review of the decisions of the board of general appraisers upon the rate and amount of duties upon imported merchandise,[7] or under the act providing for the condemnation of land for national use,[8] or under the act to prevent unlawful occupancy of public lands,[9] or under the act regulating immigration and alien contract labor,[10] or under the act providing for suits in certain cases against the United States.[11]

[1] Revised Statutes, section 629.
[2] Revised Statutes, 945, section 692; 29 Statutes at Large, 692, 695.
[3] Revised Statutes, 957; 28 Statutes at Large, 965; 29 Statutes at Large, 694.
[4] Revised Statutes, 1012.
[5] 24 Statutes at Large, 380; 25 Statutes at Large, 855.
[6] 26 Statutes at Large, 209.
[7] 26 Statutes at Large, 131.
[8] 25 Statutes at Large, 357.
[9] 23 Statutes at Large, 321.
[10] 26 Statutes at Large, 1084.
[11] 24 Statutes at Large, 505.

XIII. It thus appears that jurisdiction is conferred on the circuit courts by two classes of statutes: the one including the various acts of congress which deal with special subjects and confer jurisdiction in connection therewith, either exclusive or concurrent with the state courts, and the other including the general statutes which, after creating the circuit courts, define, extend or limit the jurisdiction thereof, and which provide the methods for invoking the federal jurisdiction, either by original proceedings or by removal from the state courts, and are known as the judiciary acts; such as the acts of September 24, 1789,[1] of July 27, 1866,[2] of March 2, 1867,[3] of March 3, 1875,[4] of March 3, 1887,[5] and of August 13, 1888.[6]

[1] 1 Statutes at Large, 73.
[2] 14 Statutes at Large, 306.
[3] 14 Statutes at Large, 558.
[4] 18 Statutes at Large, 470.
[5] 24 Statutes at Large, 552.
[6] 25 Statutes at Large, 443.

XIV. The acts of 1866 and 1867, which dealt only with the subject of the removal of cases brought in state courts, have been superseded or repealed by the later acts, and the act of 1887 is merged in the amendatory act of 1888, so that the act of 1789, with the amendments thereto, re-enacted as title XIII of the Revised Statutes, and the acts of 1875 and 1888, are the ones now in force, in whole or in part, and to which reference is to be made in determining the extent of federal jurisdiction, in addition to that created by acts of congress dealing with special subjects.

Under the provisions of the judiciary acts now

in force, jurisdiction is conferred in two general classes of cases, in one of which jurisdiction depends upon the citizenship or alienage of the parties, and which includes controversies of a civil nature wherein the matter in dispute exceeds the sum or value of $2,000, exclusive of interest and costs, and which are between citizens of different states or between a citizen of a state of the Union and foreign states, citizens or subjects, to which class may be added suits wherein the United States is plaintiff, of which jurisdiction exists without reference to the amount involved in the controversy.[1] In the second class are included all suits of a civil nature wherein the amount in controversy exceeds in sum or value the sum of $2,000, exclusive of interest and costs, and arising under the constitution, laws or treaties of the United States, and cases, without reference to the amount or value involved, wherein citizens of the same state claims lands under grants from different states.

United States v. Sayward, 160 U. S., 493.

XV. Under the first of these classes, jurisdiction does not exist when the adversary parties are both aliens,[1] or where the party plaintiff or defendant is not a citizen of a state, but is a citizen of a territory or of the District of Columbia,[2] or in cases wherein the plaintiff is a state.[3]

[1] Mossman v. Higginson, 4 Dall., 12; Jackson v. Twentyman, 2 Peters, 136; Breedlove v. Nicolet, 7 Peters, 413.

[2] Hepburn v. Ellery, 2 Cranch, 445; New Orleans v. Winter,

1 Wheat., 91; Barney v. Baltimore, 6 Wall., 280; Cameron v. Hodges. 127 U. S., 322.

³ Stone v. South Carolina, 117 U. S., 430; Upshur Co. v. Rich, 135 U. S., 467.

XVI. In cases wherein the suit is properly brought in the name of one who acts in a representative capacity, such as an executor, administrator, trustee or the like, it is the citizenship of the representative party that decides the question of jurisdiction and not that of the beneficiaries; and if the jurisdiction in a given case properly attaches when the suit is brought, subsequent changes in the parties thereto, as by substituting an executor or administrator for a deceased party or a trustee, receiver, assignee or other successor or representative for an original party in interest, will not affect or defeat the jurisdiction already acquired.

Childress v. Emory, 8 Wheat., 642; Coal Co. v. Blatchford, 11 Wall., 172; Rice v. Houston, 13 Wall., 66.

XVII. In determining whether a case is within federal jurisdiction by reason of the diverse citizenship of the adversary parties, the court may disregard merely formal parties; that is, parties having no interest in the controversy and against whom no relief is sought or is grantable under the pleadings.

Wood v. Davis, 18 How., 467; Walden v. Skinner, 101 U. S., 577; Bacon v. Rives, 106 U. S., 99.

XVIII. In the second class of cases, in which jurisdiction is conferred upon the circuit courts by the general provisions of the judiciary acts, are included cases wherein citizens of the same state claim lands under grants from different states, and in which jurisdiction exists without reference to the amount or value involved therein, and cases arising under the constitution, laws and treaties of the United States, wherein the matter in dispute exceeds in value the sum of $2,000, exclusive of interest and costs.

United States v. Sayward, 160 U. S., 493.

XIX. The jurisdiction included within the phrase — cases arising under the constitution, laws and treaties of the United States — is also divisible into two general classes; the one, which may be designated as jurisdiction direct or primary, includes cases wherein the cause of action springs directly from, or is based immediately upon, some provision of the federal constitution, laws or treaties, and the other, which may be designated as jurisdiction derivative or secondary, includes cases wherein the cause of action is not directly based upon any provision of the constitution, laws or treaties of the United States, but may be based upon a statute of a state or arise out of the principles of the common law or of equity, but wherein the right to maintain suit in a federal court is derived from the fact that the participants in the transaction giving rise to the cause of action, whether persons or corporations, acted under some right, power, duty or franchise created or conferred by the federal constitution, laws or treaties.

Thus it is held that causes of action arising out

of the acts of officers or agents of the United States in connection with the performance of their duties are based upon the laws of the United States, because those laws are the sources of their authority.[1]

So, also, it is held that causes of action based upon acts of corporations created under the laws of the United States arise under those laws, because to them the corporations owe their existence and their right and ability to act.[2]

[1] Mayer v. Cooper, 6 Wall., 247; Feibelman v. Packard, 109 U. S., 421; Baehrack v. Norton, 132 U. S., 337; Bock v. Perkins, 139 U. S., 628.

[2] Osborn v. United States Bank, 9 Wheat., 738; Pacific Railroad Removal Cases, 115 U. S., 1; Ryder v. Holt, 128 U. S., 525; Southern Kansas Ry. Co. v. Briscoe, 144 U. S., 133.

XX. In cases wherein federal jurisdiction is based upon the fact that the controversy arises under the constitution, laws or treaties of the United States, it is not necessary that diverse citizenship should exist between the adversary parties, but the circuit court may entertain jurisdiction in such suits between citizens of the same state, or between aliens or between a state and aliens, or citizens of the same or other states, provided the controversy involves the requisite amount.

Cohen v. Virginia, 6 Wheat., 264; Ames v. Kansas, 111 U. S., 419.

XXI. Jurisdiction over suits in equity may be conferred upon the circuit courts by the removal thereof from the courts of the several states. The provisions of the statute authorizing removals are to be found in the second and third sections of the act of 1888. When a case is removed into a federal court, under the provisions of the act, if it be one which properly belongs in equity, the court will order it to be entered on the equity docket, and will cause the pleadings to be reformed if necessary, in order to conform the same to the requirements of the equity practice, and the case will thenceforth be governed by the rules that would be applicable in case the suit had been commenced in the federal court by original process.

CHAPTER III.

PLACE OF BRINGING SUIT — DISTRICT — DIVISION.

XXII. If upon due consideration it appears that the case is one wherein the jurisdiction of a circuit court of the United States, sitting as a court in equity, can be rightfully invoked, then consideration must be given to the question of the federal judicial district within which the suit can be properly instituted and maintained.

The original judiciary act of 1789 provided that no civil suit shall be brought against an inhabitant of the United States, by any original process, in any other district than that whereof he is an inhabitant, or in which he shall be found at the time of serving the writ.

The judiciary act of 1875 enacted that no civil suit shall be brought against any person by any original process or proceeding in any other district than that whereof he is an inhabitant, or in which he shall be found at the time of serving such process or commencing such proceeding, except in cases enumerated in the eighth section of the act, being those brought to enforce a legal or equitable lien upon, or claim to, or to remove any incumbrance or lien or cloud upon the title to real or personal property, wherein the suit may be brought in the district wherein the property is situated.

The judiciary act of 1888 amends the first section

of the act of 1875 by enacting that, in cases wherein the federal and state courts have concurrent jurisdiction, no civil action shall be brought in a circuit court of the United States against any person by any original process or proceeding in any other district than that whereof he is an inhabitant, except where the jurisdiction is founded only on the fact that the action is between citizens of different states, in which cases the suit may be brought in the district of the residence of either plaintiff or defendant.

The act of 1888 expressly declares that its provisions are not applicable to section 8 of the act of 1875, and the jurisdiction therein created remains unaffected.

In United States v. Mooney, 116 U. S., 104, it was held by the supreme court that the act of 1875 was not intended to interfere with prior statutes conferring jurisdiction upon the circuit and district courts in special cases and over particular subjects, and the same construction was placed on the act of 1888 in the case of In re Louisville Underwriters, 134 U. S., 488.

In the case of In re Hohorst, 150 U. S., 653, it was decided that the clause of the act of 1888 limiting the right to bring suits to the district whereof the defendant is an inhabitant, or to the districts wherein the plaintiff or defendant reside in case the federal jurisdiction is based solely upon the diverse citizenship of the adversary parties, applies only to so much of the jurisdiction of the circuit courts of the United States as is concurrent with the jurisdiction of the state courts, and does not apply to cases wherein the federal jurisdiction is exclusive or wherein the controversy is between citizens of a state and foreign states, citizens or subjects.

XXIII. From the construction thus given to the several statutes regulating this subject, the rules governing the district within which suits may be brought, briefly stated, are as follows:

In cases which, from the subject-matter and the relief sought with regard thereto, are local in their nature, the suit must be brought in the district wherein the property sought to be reached or affected is situated, and this rule is applicable to the class of cases named in the eighth section of the judiciary act of 1875, being those brought to enforce a legal or equitable lien upon, or claim to, or to remove any incumbrance or lien or cloud upon the title to real or personal property.

Massie v. Watts, 6 Cranch, 148; McKenna v. Fisk, 1 How., 210; Northern Indiana R. R. Co. v. Michigan Central R. R. Co., 15 How., 232; Casey v. Adams, 102 U. S., 66.

In cases wherein the special statute of the United States creating a right and prescribing a remedy or conferring the jurisdiction over the subject-matter also enacts that suit must be brought in a named court or district, the place of bringing suit will be that defined in the particular statute.

In cases wherein the plaintiff is a citizen of a state of the Union and the defendant is a foreign state, citizen or subject, suit may be brought in any district wherein the defendant may be found for purposes of service of process.

In re Hohorst, 150 U. S., 653.

In cases wherein the controversy is between citizens of different states and the federal jurisdiction is based solely on the diverse citizenship of the adversary parties, suit may be brought in the district wherein either the plaintiff or defendant resides.

McCormick Co. v. Walthers, 134 U. S., 41; Shaw v. Quincy Mining Co., 145 U. S., 444.

In cases wherein a foreign state, citizen or subject sues a citizen of a state of the Union, the suit must be brought in the district wherein the defendant resides; and the same rule applies in cases wherein the federal jurisdiction is based upon the fact that the controversy arises under the constitution, laws or treaties of the United States, except where the statute of the United States creating the right of action or providing a remedy specially defines the court or district wherein the remedy by action must be brought.

Where the controversy is between citizens of the same state claiming land under grants from different states, suit must be brought in the district wherein the defendant resides, unless the proceeding is practically *in rem* and therefore local in its nature, in which case the suit must be in the district wherein the realty is situated.

In cases brought for the infringement of letters patent under the provisions of the act of March 3, 1897, suit may be brought in the district of which the defendant is an inhabitant, or in any district in which the defendant, whether a person, partnership or corporation, shall have committed acts of infringement, and have a regular and established place of business.

29 Statutes at Large, 695.

XXIV. A corporation created under the laws of a state of the Union is held to reside only in the state under whose laws it is created,[1] and in case there are two or more districts in the state, to be a resident of the district in the state wherein its principal place of business is located.[2] By engaging in business in other states it does not acquire a residence therein or become an inhabitant thereof.

[1] Bank of Augusta v. Earle, 13 Peters, 519; Lafayette Gas Co. v. French, 18 How., 404; Shaw v. Quincy Mining Co., 145 U. S., 444; Southern Pacific Co. v. Denton, 146 U. S., 202.
[2] Galveston, etc., Ry. Co. v. Gonzales, 151 U. S., 496.

XXV. A corporation created under the laws of a foreign country cannot become an inhabitant or resident of a state of the Union, but it may be sued in any district wherein valid service of process can be had.

In re Hohorst, 150 U. S., 653; Galveston, etc., Ry. Co. v. Gonzales, 151 U. S., 496.

XXVI. The right to insist that a suit which is within federal jurisdiction in equity must be brought within a particular district is a privilege personal to the defendant, which he may waive at his pleasure, and by appearing generally, or by pleading to the merits, either by motion, demurrer, plea or answer, he will be deemed to have waived the right to insist that suit has been brought in the wrong district.

St. Louis, etc., Ry. Co. v. McBride, 141 U. S., 127; Texas & Pacific Ry. Co. v. Cox, 145 U. S., 593; Southern Pacific Ry. Co. v. Denton, 146 U. S., 202; Trust Co. v. McGeorge, 151 U. S., 129; Interior Construction Co. v. Gibney, 160 U. S., 217.

XXVII. So far the question of the place of bringing suit has been considered with relation to cases wherein there is but one party plaintiff and one party defendant, or, if more than one, wherein all the parties on one side are citizens and residents of the one state and district, and the parties of the other side are citizens and residents of another state and district.

Cases arise, however, in which the essential parties on one side or the other are not citizens or residents of the same state and district, although of diverse citizenship from the adversary parties.

The rule in such cases is that where the federal jurisdiction is based upon the diverse citizenship of the adversary parties, and the place of bringing suit is limited to the districts wherein one or the other party reside, the words "plaintiff" and "defendant" are used in a collective sense and include all persons interested on that side of the controversy. If, therefore, it is sought to bring suit against more than one defendant, and to base the right to maintain the action in a given district upon the ground of the residence of the party defendant, all of the defendants must reside in the district wherein suit is brought.

So, also, if it is proposed to bring suit on behalf of several plaintiffs and to base the right to maintain the action in a given district upon the ground of the residence of the party plaintiff, all the plaintiffs must be residents of the district wherein suit is brought.

Several parties plaintiff, residing in different states or districts, may unite in a suit against a single defendant or several defendants residing in the same district, if the suit be brought in the district wherein the defendant or defendants reside.

A single plaintiff or several parties plaintiff residing in the same district may bring suit in the district wherein he or they reside against one or any number of defendants residing in other states.

Strawbridge v. Curtiss, 3 Cranch, 267; Peninsular Iron Co. v. Stone, 121 U. S., 631; Smith v. Lyon, 133 U. S., 315.

XXVIII. In cases wherein federal jurisdiction is not based upon the diverse citizenship of the adversary parties, and in which cases there are two or more defendants residing in different districts of the same state, suit may be brought in either district wherein a defendant resides against all the defendants residing in the state, and duplicate writs may be issued and served upon the defendants residing in the other districts.¹ And in suits of a local nature, wherein the defendant or one or more of the defendants resides in a different district in the same state from that in which the suit is brought, a writ may be issued and be served upon the defendant or defendants in the districts wherein he or they reside.²

In suits of a local nature, wherein the land or subject matter lies partly in two or more districts in the same state, suit may be brought in either district, and the court has jurisdiction to decide the controversy fully, and to issue and execute process the same as though the property were wholly in one district.³

¹ Revised Statutes, section 740.
² Revised Statutes, section 741.
³ Revised Statutes, section 742.

XXIX. To obviate the difficulties that would ensue under the foregoing rules, in cases wherein there are several parties in interest who are not residents of the same state, it is enacted in section 737 of the Revised Statutes that where there are several defendants and one or more of them are neither inhabitants of nor found within the district in which the suit is brought, and do not voluntarily appear, the court may entertain jurisdiction and proceed to trial and adjudication of the suit between the parties who are properly before it, but the judgment or decree rendered therein shall not conclude or prejudice other parties not regularly served with process nor voluntarily appearing to answer; and the non-joinder of parties who are not inhabitants of nor found within the district shall not constitute matter of abatement or objection to the suit; and in equity rule 47 it is provided that in all cases where it shall appear that persons, who might otherwise be deemed necessary or proper parties to the suit, cannot be made parties thereto by reason of being out of the jurisdiction of the court, or because their joinder would oust the jurisdiction of the court as to the parties before the court, or if for any reason they cannot be made parties, the court may in its discretion proceed in the cause without making such persons parties, the decree being without prejudice to their rights.[1]

In construing this section of the statutes and the equity rule, it is held by the supreme court that the provisions thereof do not enable a court to dispense with the presence of parties whose interests are so connected with the subject of the controversy that a decree cannot be entered without affecting their interests, or leaving the controversy in such a condition that its termination, by any decree that might be entered, would be inconsistent with equity and good conscience.[2]

[1] Williams v. United States, 138 U. S., 514.
[2] Shields v. Barrow, 17 How., 129; Barney v. Baltimore City, 6 Wall., 284; Ribon v. Railroad Companies, 16 Wall., 446; Kendig v. Dean, 97 U. S., 425; Gregory v. Stetson, 133 U. S., 579.

XXX. In some districts, divisions therein are created by act of congress, and the statute defines the division wherein suit should be brought, the general rule being to require that suits not local in character must be brought in the division wherein the defendant resides, or, if there are several defendants residing in different divisions, then suit may be brought in any division wherein a defendant resides, and in suits of a local character the same must be brought in the division wherein the property or some part of it is situated.

To ascertain the rule, in this particular, obtaining in a given district, reference must be made to the act of congress creating the divisions in that district.

CHAPTER IV.

MODE OF BRINGING SUIT — FORM OF BILL — JURISDICTIONAL AVERMENTS.

XXXI. The initial step in bringing a suit in equity is the preparation and filing of the bill, the introductory part of which should be substantially in the following form:

In the Circuit Court of the United States in and for the —— District of ——.

—— Term, 18—.

A. B.
v.   } Equity.
C. D. and E. F.

To the Judges of the Circuit Court of the United States for the —— District of ——.

A. B., a citizen of the state of ——, residing in —— county in said state, brings this his bill against C. D., a citizen of the state of ——, residing in —— county in said state, and E. F., a citizen of the state of ——, residing in —— county in said state. And thereupon this complainant avers and says, etc.

XXXII. From the fact that the courts of the United States are of limited jurisdiction, it follows that the existence of jurisdiction should be made plain upon the face of the record in each case.

Therefore whether jurisdiction in the federal court over a given cause is claimed to exist by reason of the diverse citizenship, or alienage and citizenship, of the adversary parties, or by reason of the subject-matter of the controversy, the facts relied on as showing the existence of the federal jurisdiction in equity in the court and district wherein the suit is brought should be made clear upon the face of the bill, or the same will be demurrable, or may be dismissed by the court of its own motion.

<small>Hornthal v. Collector, 9 Wall., 560; Godfrey v. Terry, 97 U. S., 171; Mansfield R. R. Co. v. Swan, 111 U. S., 379; Hancock v. Holbrook, 112 U. S., 229; Insurance Co. v. Rhoads, 119 U. S., 237; Everhart v. Huntsville College, 120 U. S., 223; Cameron v. Hodges, 127 U. S., 322; Stevens v. Nichols, 130 U. S., 230; Tyler v. Savage, 143 U. S., 79; Hanford v. Davies, 163 U. S., 273.</small>

XXXIII. In cases wherein suit may be brought only in the district wherein the defendant resides, or wherein suit may be brought in the district wherein either plaintiff or defendant resides, and the suit is instituted in a state wherein there are two or more federal districts, it is not sufficient to aver solely that the party is a citizen of the state, but in addition thereto the averment must show that the party resides in the district wherein suit is brought, which may be done by averring that the party resides within the district, naming it, or by averring the place of his residence to be within a named county, and the court will take judicial knowledge of the fact that the named county forms part of the district.

XXXIV. A corporation cannot be or become a citizen of a state;[1] and for jurisdictional purposes a suit by or against a corporation is deemed to be a suit in favor of, or against, the stockholders therein, who are conclusively held to be citizens of the state under whose laws the corporation is created.[2]

When, therefore, a corporation is a party, it is not sufficient to simply aver that the corporation is a citizen of a named state, but the corporate name should be set forth, followed by the averment that the same "is a corporation created under the laws of the state of ——, and having its principal place of business at ——."[3]

[1] Paul v. Virginia, 8 Wall., 168; Ducat v. Chicago, 10 Wall., 410.

[2] Louisville R. R. Co. v. Letson, 2 How., 497; Muller v. Dows, 94 U. S., 444.

[3] Lafayette Ins. Co. v. French, 18 How., 404; Railroad Co. v. Harris, 12 Wall., 65; Ex parte Schollenberger, 96 U. S., 369; Pennsylvania Co. v. Railroad Co., 118 U. S., 290; Goodlet v. Railroad Co., 122 U. S., 391.

XXXV. In cases wherein a copartnership or association other than a corporation is a party, the names of the individuals composing the same must be set forth, with the proper averment of their citizenship, as it is not permissible to declare in favor of or against a copartnership or association in the firm name,[1] and the given names of the parties in all cases should be used instead of the initial only.[2]

Residence and citizenship are not synonymous terms, and, to show jurisdiction, the averment must be that of citizenship.[3]

[1] The Protector, 11 Wall., 82; Moore v. Simonds, 100 U. S., 145; Chapman v. Barney, 129 U. S., 677.

[2] Monroe Cattle Co. v. Becker, 147 U. S., 47.

[3] Parker v. Overman, 18 How., 137; Robertson v. Case, 97 U. S., 646; Grace v. American Central Ins. Co., 109 U. S., 278; Anderson v. Watt, 138 U. S., 694; Finmour v. Elyton Land Co., 139 U. S., 398; Southern Pacific R. R. Co. v. Denton, 146 U. S., 202; Wolfe v. Insurance Co., 148 U. S., 389.

XXXVI. The facts constituting the cause of action should be set forth concisely, yet clearly, avoiding all unnecessary recitals of deeds, documents, contracts, or other instruments *in hæc verba*, or of matters of mere evidence.

It is not necessary to include a clause averring a confederacy between the defendants to injure or defraud the complainant, unless such confederation constitutes, in the particular case, one of the grounds relied upon by complainant for the relief sought; nor a clause setting forth the matters or excuses which the defendant is supposed to rely upon by way of defense; but the complainant may, when desirable, state in his bill any matter which he may suppose the defendant will rely upon, and avoid the effect thereof by making proper counter averments thereto; nor a clause averring that the acts complained of are contrary to equity, and that complainant is remediless at law.

If the facts averred in setting forth the cause of action show a case of equitable cognizance, then a formal averment that the party is without remedy at law is merely surplusage; whereas if the facts averred do not show that the party has no adequate and complete remedy at law, then a formal averment to that end is ineffectual to show the fact, being the averment of a mere conclusion of law.

Rule 21.

XXXVII. If any persons, other than those named in the bill as defendants, should appear to be necessary or proper parties, the reason why they are not made parties should be averred; as, for instance, that they are without the jurisdiction of the court, or cannot be joined without ousting the jurisdiction as to the other parties.

If desired, the bill may contain a prayer that if the absent parties should come within the jurisdiction, process may issue to bring them into the suit.

Rule 22.

XXXVIII. If a preliminary injunction, writ of *ne exeat* or other special process or order pending the suit is sought for, the reasons or grounds upon which the same is asked should be set forth, with a special prayer for the issuance of such process.

Rule 21.

XXXIX. The bill must also contain a prayer for the issuance of the process by subpœna, in which prayer must be included the names of all the defendants named as such in the introductory part of the bill.[1]

If any of the defendants are minors, or otherwise under guardianship or incompetent, the fact should be stated, in order that proper service may be had and such other action be taken as is necessary for the protection of the rights of such party.[1]

XL. The bill concludes with the prayers for relief, which must include the special relief sought by complainant, and also a prayer for general relief.[2] Under the latter there can be properly granted only relief conformable to the case made in the bill, and therefore care should be taken to include within the special prayer all the relief to which the complainant may be entitled under the facts of the case.[3]

There must be annexed to the bill the signature of one of the counsel for complainant, which signing is deemed to be an affirmation on his part that upon the instructions given to him and the case laid before him there is good ground for the suit in the manner in which it is set forth in the bill.[4]

It is not required that the bill shall be sworn to or be supported by affidavit, unless some special order or process, pending the suit, is asked for, such as a preliminary injunction or writ of *ne exeat* or other like matter.

[1] Rule 23.
[2] Rule 21.
[3] Tyler v. Savage, 143 U. S., 79; Kent v. Canal Co., 144 U. S., 75.
[4] Rule 24.

XLI. Since the adoption of the amendment to rule 40, declaring that it shall not be necessary to interrogate a defendant specially upon any statement in the bill, unless complainant desires to do so for the purposes of discovery, and of the statute permitting and compelling parties in interest to testify as witnesses, the use of special interrogatories as part of the bill as a means of discovery has largely fallen into disuse, rendering it unnecessary to notice the rules regulating the form and particulars thereof, otherwise than by reference to rules 40–44 inclusive.

XLII. If the averments of the bill show that the injuries complained of have been of long standing, so that laches may be imputed to complainant in not sooner moving for the protection of his rights, the facts relied on as excusing the delay should be set forth in the bill, or otherwise it may be attacked by demurrer or plea, or the court may of its own motion refuse to consider the case.

Thus, if suit could not be earlier brought by reason of the absence of defendant, or of some disability on part of complainant, or because defendant fraudulently kept the facts concealed, or because complainant, without fault, was ignorant of his rights, or if any other reason exists excusing the delay, the facts should be averred in the bill, and thus the apparent laches on part of complainant be explained.

Badger v. Badger, 2 Wall., 87; Hume v. Beal, 17 Wall., 336; Marsh v. Whitmore, 21 Wall., 178; Sullivan v. Railroad Co., 94 U. S., 806; Hayward v. National Bank, 96 U. S., 611; Speidel v. Henrici, 120 U. S., 377; Richards v. Mackal, 124 U. S., 183; Mackall v. Casilear, 137 U. S., 556; Martin v. Gray, 142 U. S., 236; Foster v. Railroad Co., 146 U. S., 88; Lane & B. Co. v. Locke, 150 U. S., 193; Halstead v. Grinnan, 152 U. S., 412; Willard v. Wood, 164 U. S., 502.

XLIII. Where one or more stockholders in a corporation bring a bill against the corporation and other parties for the enforcement or protection of rights ordinarily assertable by the corporation as the representative of all the stockholders, on the ground that the corporation fails or refuses to act in the premises, such bill must be verified, and must show that the complainant was a shareholder at the time of the transaction of which he complains, or that his share had since devolved on him by operation of law; that the suit is not collusively brought in the name of the stockholder as a means of conferring jurisdiction on the United States court, and must also set forth with particularity the efforts made by complainant to secure action by the directors or trustees, and if necessary by the shareholders, and the cause of failure in securing action through the corporation.

Rule 94. Hawes v. Oakland, 104 U. S., 450; Huntington v. Palmer, 104 U. S., 482; Quincy v. Steele, 120 U. S., 241; Porter v. Sabin, 149 U. S., 473.

CHAPTER V.

OF THE PARTIES.

XLIV. As to parties, the general rule is that all persons interested in or to be affected by the results of the litigation should be made parties plaintiff or defendant, to the end that the one proceeding and the one decree may settle and adjudicate the entire controversy.[1]

Where it appears, however, that one or more of those interested cannot be made parties, by reason of being without the jurisdiction of the court, or for other good reason, or because making them parties would oust the jurisdiction of the court, the cause may proceed without their presence, provided the interest of those made parties is such that the court can consistently hear and determine the issues as to them; but in such cases the decree cannot prejudice the rights of those not made parties.[2]

So, also, where the parties on either side are very numerous, and cannot, without manifest inconvenience and delay, be all brought in as parties, the suit may proceed if sufficient parties to represent all the adverse interests are brought before the court.[3]

Where, upon the face of the bill, it appears that persons not made parties are interested in the suit, the reasons why they are not made parties should be set forth in the bill.

If the interest of those not made parties is such that a final decree cannot be entered without injuriously affecting such interest, or leaving the controversy in such condition as may be inconsistent with equity, the court will require such absent parties to be brought in, and if this cannot be done will dismiss the bill.[4] If doubt exists whether the court will grant a final decree by reason of the absence of parties, the question should, if possible, be presented and settled before incurring the delay and expense of taking testimony.

[1] Russell v. Clark's Ex'r, 7 Cranch, 74; Caldwell v. Taggart, 4 Pet., 190; Shields v. Barrow, 17 How., 130; Williams v. Bankhead, 19 Wall., 563; McArthur v. Scott, 113 U. S., 340.

[2] Mulligan v. Milledge, 3 Cranch, 220; Elmendorf v. Taylor, 10 Wheaton, 153; Mallow v. Hinde, 12 Wheaton, 193; Payne v. Hook, 7 Wall., 425; Traders' Bank v. Campbell, 14 Wall., 87; Keller v. Ashford, 133 U. S., 610; McGahan v. Bank of Rondout, 156 U. S., 218.

[3] Mandeville v. Riggs, 2 Pet., 482; Williams v. Bankhead, 19 Wall., 563.

[4] Riddle v. Mandeville, 5 Cranch, 322; Russell v. Clark's Ex'r, 7 Cranch, 74; Marshall v. Beverly, 5 Wheaton, 313; Mallow v. Hinde, 12 Wheaton, 193; Barney v. Baltimore, 6 Wall., 280; Bank v. Railroad Co., 11 Wall., 624; Traders' Bank v. Campbell, 14 Wall., 87; Ribon v. Railroad Co., 16 Wall., 446.

XLV. Persons incapable of instituting suits for themselves may sue by guardian or *prochein ami*, and a guardian *ad litem* may be appointed by the court or judge to defend on behalf of such incapables.

Rule 87.

XLVI. In suits upon joint and several demands, including those against principals and sureties, the complainant may at his option proceed against one or more of those severally liable.[1]

In suits to enforce the execution of the trusts of a will it is not necessary to make the heir at law a party, unless it is desired to establish the will against him.[2]

Where real estate is vested in trustees by devise, with power to sell and to collect and receipt for the rents and profits, such trustees, for purposes of suit, represent the beneficiaries to the same extent as administrators or executors represent the persons interested in the personal estate, and such beneficiaries, interested in the realty or the rents and profits thereof, need not be made parties unless the court shall so order.[3]

So, also, where trustees represent the beneficiaries in regard to the general interest in the trust property, so that their acts touching the property bind the beneficiaries, the trustees alone may be made parties to suits affecting the trust property.

[1] Rule 51.
[2] Rule 50.
[3] Rule 49. Kerrison v. Stewart, 93 U. S., 155; Corcoran v. Canal Co., 94 U. S., 741; Shaw v. Railroad Co., 100 U. S., 605; Richter v. Jerome, 123 U. S., 233.

CHAPTER VI.

MESNE PROCESS — ISSUANCE — SERVICE.

XLVII. The ordinary process issued to bring the defendants into court is a subpœna, which is issued by the clerk upon the filing of the bill in his office, and at the option of the complainant may be made returnable at the first or second rule day next ensuing, occurring after twenty days from date of the issuance of the process.

If there are more than one defendant, separate subpœnas for each, or a joint subpœna for all, may be issued at the election of complainant, save in cases wherein a husband and wife are defendants, against whom the subpœna must be joint.

When the bill is filed a *præcipe* must also be filed with the clerk, directing the issuance of a subpœna or subpœnas as desired, and naming the rule day to which process is to be made returnable.

Rules 7, 11, 12.

XLVIII. When issued, the subpœna is served by the marshal, his deputy or by some other person specially appointed by the court, or by a judge thereof, when necessity for such appointment exists.

In case of service by an appointee, return of service must be made under oath.

Rule 15. Revised Statutes, section 922.

XLIX. Service is made by delivering a copy of the subpœna to the defendant personally, or by leaving a copy thereof at the dwelling-house or usual place of abode of each defendant, with some adult person who is a member of, or resident in, the family of the defendant.

Rule 13.

L. If a subpœna is returned not served upon a defendant, the complainant is entitled to other subpœnas against such defendant, until due service is made.

Rule 14.

LI. When a suit in equity is commenced, and satisfactory proof is made to the circuit court, or to the circuit justice or judge, that the defendant designs quickly to depart from the United States; that there is due from him a sum certain or capable of reduction to certainty; that complainant has no sufficient legal redress, and that irreparable injury or a denial of justice will be caused to complainant if the defendant so departs, such court or judge may order the issuance of a writ of *ne exeat*, upon which the marshal arrests the defendant and keeps him in custody, unless he gives security to abide the order and decree of the court.

Revised Statutes, section 717; Griswold v. Hazard, 141 U. S., 260.

LII. In suits to enforce a lien upon, or claim to, or to remove any incumbrance, lien or cloud upon, the title to real or personal property within the district wherein the suit is brought, if one or more of the defendants shall not be an inhabitant of or found within the district, service may be made by procuring from the court an order directing such defendant to appear, plead, answer or demur by a day to be fixed in the order, which order shall be served on such defendant wherever found, and also upon the person or persons in possession or charge of the property, if any there be. If personal service of such order cannot be made upon such defendant, the same may be published, in such manner as the court may direct, not less than once a week for six consecutive weeks.

To procure such order, a motion in writing should be filed, accompanied with an affidavit stating briefly the nature of the suit, the names of the defendants upon whom service cannot be had within the district, and the place of their supposed residence.

Upon proof being filed showing service of publication of the order as directed by the court, jurisdiction attaches so as to enable the court to adjudicate touching the property involved in said suit and to bind the interest of the absent party in the same, subject to the right of such party to appear within one year from the entry of final judgment, and, upon motion, to have such judgment against him opened and the matter reheard.

18 Statutes at Large, 472.

LIII. When a subpœna, order or other process is to be served without the limits of the district wherein suit is brought, it should be placed in the hands of the marshal within whose district service is to be made, unless some other person has been appointed to make service.

LIV. The marshal or person charged with the duty of making service of the subpœna should make the same forthwith, and when made should at once return the process to the clerk's office whence it issued, and, upon return of service being made, the clerk must enter the suit upon his docket as pending in the court, stating the time of such entry.

Rule 16. Warren Co. v. Marcy, 97 U. S., 96; Union Trust Co. v. Navigation Co., 130 U. S., 565.

CHAPTER VII.

DEFAULT AND DECREE PRO CONFESSO.

LV. If a defendant, having been duly served, fails to enter an appearance at the proper time, or having appeared fails to file a plea, demurrer or answer to the bill by the proper rule day, the complainant may enter an order that the bill be taken *pro confesso*.

Thereupon the cause may be proceeded in *ex parte*, and, after the expiration of thirty days from the entry of default, decree therein may be entered, or the complainant, if he requires an answer to enable him to obtain a proper decree, may procure process by attachment against such defendant, upon which process the defendant may be arrested and held until he fully complies with the order of the court or judge, as to pleading to or answering said bill.

Rules 18, 19. Thomson v. Wooster, 114 U. S., 104.

CHAPTER VIII.

APPEARANCE AND PROCEEDINGS ON BEHALF OF DEFENDANT.

LVI. To prevent the entry of a default the defendant must, either personally or by his solicitor, enter his appearance at the rule day to which the process is made returnable, provided he was served with process twenty days before that day; otherwise the appearance day shall be the next rule day succeeding the day when the process is returnable.

A defendant may waive the service of process, or, being served, may waive the time allowed him and enter his appearance either personally or by his solicitor, entry thereof to be noted in the order book by the clerk.

Rules 17, 18.

LVII. Having appeared, the defendant, if cause therefor exists, may, on or before the rule day next after the return day of the process, except to the bill on the ground that it contains impertinent or scandalous matter, that is, that it contains recitals of matters not pertinent or relevant to the real cause of action, or that it contains needless repetitions rendering the bill unnecessarily prolix, or that it contains, unnecessarily, statements of a scandalous nature calculated to do injury to the persons affected thereby.

Upon exceptions of this nature being filed, the

same may be at once referred to a master. If it be found by the master, or by the court, that the exceptions are well taken, the impertinent or scandalous matter will be expunged at the expense of complainant, and he may be adjudged to pay all the costs of the defendant to that time.

When the defendant has procured an order referring such exceptions to a master, he must procure action thereon by the master by the next succeeding rule day, or the exceptions will be deemed to be abandoned, unless the master certifies that further time is needed to enable him to complete the examination.

Rules 25–27.

LVIII. Unless otherwise ordered by a judge of the court, for cause shown, the defendant, to prevent a default being entered, must file a plea, demurrer or answer to the bill on the rule day next succeeding the rule day upon which his appearance was entered.

Rules 18, 32.

LIX. The defendant may demur or plead to the whole bill or to part of it, or he may demur to part, plead to part, and answer as to the residue, or he may answer to the whole bill.

In case the bill specially charges fraud or combination on part of the defendants, a plea to such part must be accompanied with an answer fortifying the plea, and explicitly denying the fraud and combination, and the facts on which such charge is founded.

If any part of the bill is good and a demurrer to the whole bill is filed, it will be overruled.

Rule 32. Livingston v. Story, 9 Pet., 632; Buffington v. Harvey, 95 U. S., 99.

LX. No demurrer or plea shall be allowed to be filed to a bill unless accompanied by a certificate of counsel that it is in his opinion well founded in point of law, and by the affidavit of the defendant that it is not interposed for the purpose of causing delay in the progress of the suit, and, in case of a plea, the affidavit must further aver that it is true in point of fact, and unless thus supported the demurrer or plea may be disregarded.

Rule 31. Sheffield Furnace Co. v. Witherow, 149 U. S., 574.

LXI. Whenever a ground of defense is apparent on the bill itself, either from matters therein alleged, or from a failure to allege some fact or facts essential to sustain complainant's right to relief, or from defects in the frame or form of the bill, or because it appears that the lapse of time or laches of complainant have barred the right of recovery, or it appears that there is a misjoinder of parties or a want of necessary parties, or that there is a lack of jurisdiction in the court, a demurrer to the bill will lie, and usually the objection should thus be taken.

If the bill is defective in substance in not showing a sufficient original cause of action, or by showing that a sufficient defense exists or that the court is without jurisdiction, a demurrer saves the expense caused by answering and taking evidence.

If the defect is in matter of form, the failure to demur may be deemed to be a waiver of the objection.

Livingston v. Story, 9 Pet., 632; Maxwell v. Kennedy, 8 How., 210; Griffing v. Gibb, 2 Black, 519; Dillon v. Barnard, 21 Wall., 430; National Bank v. Carpenter, 101 U. S., 567.

LXII. If the court of equity has jurisdiction over the subject-matter and can grant the relief sought, the objection to the jurisdiction on the ground that there is an adequate remedy at law should be taken promptly and before entering upon a defense to the merits.

Reynes v. Dumont, 130 U. S., 354; Kilbourn v. Sunderland, 130 U. S., 505; Brown v. Lake Superior Iron Co., 134 U. S., 530; Perego v. Dodge, 163 U. S., 160.

LXIII. The demurrer may be general or special. It is the former when no particular ground is assigned, except that there is no equity in the bill. If the bill is attacked for defects in substance, the general demurrer is sufficient, though it is usual, and is the better practice, to state clearly and concisely the defects relied on as showing want of equity.

A demurrer is special when particular defects are attacked, and this form is indispensable when the objection to the bill is as to matter of form.

When a demurrer is interposed to a part only of a bill, it should show the part or parts to which it is intended to apply.

LXIV. Where the objections or defenses relied upon by the defendant do not appear upon the face of the bill, they must be raised by a plea or answer.

A plea is said to be a special answer to a bill, or some part of it, whereby it is sought to show that, by reason of the special matter in the plea set forth, the complainant is barred from maintaining suit on the matters in the bill alleged, or is stopped from further progress in the forum or form in which the suit is pending.

The main purpose of the plea is to save the delay and expense of going into the case at large when some ground exists which, when it is brought to the attention of the court, will result in the abatement of the pending suit or bar recovery therein. The defense, therefore, proper for a plea is generally one that reduces the case, or some material part of it, to a single point.

Thus, if the defense is that the court has not jurisdiction of the cause, or that the suit is barred by the statute of limitations, or that an indispensable party is not joined, or that there is pending another suit upon the same cause of action, or other single matter which, if proven, will abate or bar the suit, the same should be presented by a plea.

Livingston v. Story, 11 Pet., 351; Wickliffe v. Owings, 17 How., 47; Insurance Co. v. Brune, 96 U. S., 588; Farley v. Kittson, 120 U. S., 303.

LXV. If the bill is not demurrable, and no fact, proper to be presented by a plea, exists either as matter in abatement or in bar, then the defense must be presented by way of answer, and the defendant is entitled by answer to insist upon all matters of defense, not being merely matters of abatement, or to the character of the parties, or of form, which exist in his behalf.[1]

The defendant may in the answer suggest that the bill is defective for want of parties, and by proper averment state the names of such parties and their relation to the case.[2]

If the bill does not waive an answer under oath, the same must be sworn or affirmed to by the defendant before a judge of a court of the United States or of a state or territory, or before a commissioner appointed by the United States circuit court to take testimony, or before a master in chancery appointed by a United States circuit court or notary public.[3]

If thus sworn to, in obedience to the demand of the bill, the allegations of the answer, so far as responsive to the bill, are evidence in favor of defendant. To overcome same requires satisfactory testimony of two witnesses, or of one corroborated by circumstances equivalent in weight to that of another.[4]

[1] Rule 39. Wickliffe v. Owings, 17 How., 47.
[2] Rule 52.
[3] Rule 59.
[4] Rule 41. Seitz v. Mitchell, 94 U. S., 580; Vigel v. Hopt, 104 U. S., 441; Farley v. Kittson, 120 U. S., 303; Morrison v. Durr, 122 U. S., 518; Union R. R. Co. v. Dull, 124 U. S., 173; Southern Co. v. Silva, 125 U. S., 247.

LXVI. When a corporation is a party defendant to a bill requiring an answer under oath, the answer of the corporation should be attested by the corporate seal, that being the highest evidence that the answer is the solemn act of the corporation, and stands in place of the oath of an individual.

Bronson v. Railroad Co., 2 Wall., 283.

LXVII. The defendant may in his answer suggest that the bill is defective for want of parties, giving the names or description of such parties and the facts showing the necessity of their being made parties, and thereupon the complainant may, within fourteen days after answer filed, set down the cause for argument upon this objection only, by entering in the clerk's order book a notification to that effect.

If complainant does not thus set down the cause for argument on the objection of want of parties, but proceeds to a hearing generally, he shall not, if the objection of want of parties be sustained, be entitled as of course to an order to amend by adding the parties, but the court may, if it thinks fit, dismiss the bill.

Rule 52.

LXVIII. If the defendant does not, by plea or answer, object to the bill as defective for want of parties, the objection will not be allowed to prevail at the hearing of the cause, if the court can grant a decree saving the rights of the absent parties.

Rule 53. Bank v. Seton, 1 Pet., 299; Story v. Livingston, 13 Pet., 359; Keller v. Ashford, 133 U. S., 610.

LXIX. If the allegations of the bill, averring the character of the parties, as that they are administrators, executors, trustees, or the like, and averring the citizenship of the adversary parties, are sufficient, *prima facie*, to sustain the jurisdiction of the court and the right to sue, issue thereon, if at all, must be taken by a plea, and not by answer.

Rule 39. Wickliffe v. Owings, 17 How., 47; Farmington v. Pillsbury, 114 U. S., 143.

LXX. Since the adoption of the act of 1875 this general rule is subject to the qualification found in section 5 of that act, to the effect that if it appears in a suit at any time that it does not really and substantially involve a controversy within the jurisdiction of the court, or that the parties have been collusively made or joined for the purpose of creating a cause cognizable in the United States circuit court, such court shall proceed no farther, but must dismiss the cause.

18 Statutes at Large, 470. Williams v. Nottawa, 104 U. S., 209; Barry v. Edmunds, 116 U. S., 550; Hartog v. Memory, 116 U. S., 588.

LXXI. As already stated, the defendant may demur to part, plead to part, and answer to the residue of the bill.

It cannot be objected to the demurrer or plea that the same does not cover so much of the bill as it might, by law, have extended to, nor because the answer may extend to some part of the same matter covered by the demurrer or plea,[1] but, if the answer extends to the whole of the matter covered by the plea, the latter will be overruled.[2]

[1] Rules 32, 36, 37.
[2] Grant v. Phœnix Life Ins. Co., 121 U. S., 105.

CHAPTER VIII.

FURTHER PROCEEDINGS ON PART OF COMPLAINANT, INCLUDING REPLICATION.

LXXII. If a demurrer to a bill is filed, the complainant must, on the rule day the same is filed, or on the next succeeding rule day, set the same down for argument, or the failure so to do will be deemed an admission that the demurrer is well taken, and his bill will be dismissed, unless, upon application to a judge of the court, further time be allowed him to set the same down for hearing.

Rule 38.

LXXIII. If a plea to the bill is filed, the complainant must, on the same or by the next ensuing rule day, either set the same down for argument or file a reply to the plea.[1]

If set down for argument the facts well pleaded in the plea are admitted for the purposes of the argument, and the question of the legal sufficiency of the plea, in form and substance, is alone presented.[2]

If, upon the hearing, the plea is held good, or, in other words, is allowed, the complainant is entitled to file a reply, as he may do without setting down the plea for argument.[3]

By a reply issue is taken upon the facts alleged in the plea.

The allegations of fact in the plea, though under oath, are not evidence in favor of defendant.[2]

The taking of the evidence upon an issue of fact arising upon a plea, and reply thereto, is governed by the rules applicable to an issue arising upon an answer and replication.[4]

If, upon the hearing of the issue of fact, the finding is in favor of the defendant, the effect thereof depends upon the nature of the issue or facts determined upon the plea, the defendant being entitled to the benefit thereof only so far as in law and equity they ought to avail him.[5]

[1] Rule 33.
[2] Farley v. Kittson, 120 U. S., 303.
[3] United States v. Dalles Military Road Co., 140 U. S., 599.
[4] Hughes v. Blake, 6 Wheaton, 453.
[5] Rule 33. Pearce v. Rice, 142 U. S., 28; Horn v. Detroit Dry Dock Co., 150 U. S., 610; Green v. Bogue, 158 U. S., 478.

LXXIV. If, upon the hearing, a demurrer or plea is overruled, the complainant is entitled to costs, unless the court is satisfied that there was good ground for the interposition of the same, and that it was not interposed for delay.[1]

The defendant will also be required to answer the bill, or so much thereof as was covered by the plea or demurrer, by the next rule day or such other time as the court may deem advisable, and in default of such answer the bill may be taken *pro confesso*.[1]

If the demurrer or plea on the hearing is sustained the defendant is entitled to costs, and the court may, at its discretion, upon motion of complainant, permit him to amend his bill upon such terms as may be reasonable.[2]

[1] Rule 34. Powder Co. v. Powder Works. 98 U. S., 126.
[2] Rule 35. National Bank v. Carpenter, 101 U. S., 567.

LXXV. Upon the filing of an answer the complainant may, if cause exists, file exceptions thereto on the ground that it contains scandalous or impertinent matter.

The exceptions must be in writing, signed by counsel, and be filed by the rule day next after the day of the filing the answer.

Upon filing the same the complainant must at once apply to a judge for an order referring the exceptions to a master for examination, and without delay procure the master to examine and report thereon on the same or the next succeeding rule day, unless the master shall certify that further time is needed to enable him to complete the examination.

Rule 27.

LXXVI. Exceptions to the answer may also be filed on the ground of insufficiency.

The exceptions must be in writing, be signed by counsel, and be filed by the rule day next succeeding the rule day upon which the answer was filed, unless the court, or a judge thereof, shall, for cause shown, enlarge the time.[1]

The exceptions should point out specifically the particular parts of the bill which it is claimed are not sufficiently answered, and the defects in the answer excepted to.

Exceptions for scandal or impertinence should be disposed of before excepting on ground of insufficiency.

If a defendant demurs or pleads to any part of the discovery sought by a bill, and also answers the bill, exceptions to the answer for insufficiency should not be filed until the demurrer or plea is disposed of, as filing the same admits the validity of the demurrer or plea.

If, however, the demurrer or plea is only to the relief prayed by the bill, exceptions to the answer may be filed without thereby admitting the validity of the demurrer or plea.

If the defendant deems the exceptions well taken, he must file an amended answer by the next succeeding rule day; but if he does not, by so amending, admit the exceptions, then the complainant must set the same down for hearing on the next following rule day before a judge of the court.[2]

If not thus set down for hearing the exceptions are deemed abandoned, and the answer is deemed sufficient.[3]

If, on hearing, the exceptions are sustained, the defendant must, by the next rule day, file a full and complete answer, or the complainant may take the bill as confessed, so far as the matter excepted to in the answer applied thereto, or he may by attachment compel the defendant to make full answer to the matters covered by the exceptions.[4]

The court or a judge thereof may, for cause shown, enlarge the time for amending the answer.

[1] Rule 61.
[2] Rule 63.
[3] Rule 63.
[4] Rule 64.

LXXVII. If the complainant does not except to the answer, or if, being excepted to, the same is amended, or the exceptions upon a hearing are not sustained, and if the case is not set down for hearing on the bill and answer, the complainant must, by the rule day next succeeding the rule day upon which the answer or the amended answer is filed, file a general replication thereto, and thus complete the issue in the cause. If the replication is not thus filed, the defendant is entitled to an order, as of course, for the dismissal of the suit.

The court or a judge thereof, for cause shown, may allow a replication to be filed after the rule day upon which it should have been filed.[1]

Special replications cannot be filed.

If, by reason of matters alleged in the answer, it becomes necessary for complainant to allege new matter, it must be done by an amendment to the bill, or by a supplemental bill.[2]

[1] Rule 66.
[2] Rules 45, 57. Marsteller v. McLean, 7 Cranch, 156; Vattier v. Hinde, 7 Pet., 252.

Exceptions to the answer do not perform the office of a demurrer, in presenting the question whether the facts averred in the answer constitute a defense to the case made in the bill, and as it is not permissible to file a demurrer to an answer, if it is desired to submit the case on the questions of law arising on the answer, the only method is by setting down the case for hearing on bill and answer.[3]

[1] Rule 66.
[2] Rules 45, 57.
[3] Banks v. Manchester, 128 U. S., 244.

CHAPTER IX.

HEARING ON BILL AND ANSWER—TAKING TESTIMONY ON ISSUE JOINED—REFERENCE TO MASTER AND PROCEEDINGS BEFORE SAME.

LXXVIII. The complainant may, when the original or amended answer is filed, set the cause down for hearing upon bill and answer.

In such case, the matters well pleaded in the answer are deemed to be true as matters of fact, and the case is heard upon the allegations of fact in the bill contained, and not denied in the answer, taken in connection with the facts averred in the answer.

Rule 41. Leeds v. Insurance Co., 2 Wheaton, 380; Banks v. Manchester, 128 U. S., 244.

LXXIX. A cause being at issue upon questions of fact, two general modes exist for submitting such issue for final determination; *i. e.*, the evidence may be taken and the cause be submitted in the first instance to the court, or by consent of parties the same may be sent to a master for his examination and report.

LXXX. If the cause is not referred to a master, ninety days from the time the issue is joined are allowed for the taking of the testimony on behalf of both parties, unless the court or a judge thereof, for good cause shown, shall enlarge the time.

Rule 69. Ingle v. Jones, 9 Wall., 486.

LXXXI. Either party may give notice to the other that he desires the evidence to be taken orally, in which event all the witnesses must be examined before one of the examiners of the court, or before an examiner specially named by the court to act in the given case, who must be furnished with a copy of the bill and answer.

The parties have a right to be present at the examination, and the witnesses are examined and cross-examined in the mode usual in common-law courts. The testimony given must be taken down in form of question and answer, unless parties consent that same be taken in narrative form. When completed, each deposition must be read over to the witness giving the same, and be by him signed in the presence of the parties or their counsel. If a witness refuses to sign a deposition the examiner may do so, and thus authenticate the same.

Objections made to questions or answers must be noted down upon the deposition by the examiner, as he does not possess the power to decide upon the competency, relevancy or materiality of the questions.

When the evidence is to be thus taken orally, the court may, upon motion of either party, assign the time within which the complainant shall take his evidence in support of the bill, and a time thereafter for the defendant to take his evidence, and a time thereafter for complainant's evidence in reply; and the evidence of the respective parties must be so taken, unless the parties by agreement, or the court on motion and for cause, shall extend the time therefor.

If either party has any documentary evidence not introduced before the examiner in connection with the testimony of the witnesses, he should file the same with the clerk of the court within the time allowed him for taking evidence orally.

The examiner may fix, by order, the time and place for conducting the examination of the several witnesses, and notice thereof must be given by the counsel of the moving party to the adversary party or his counsel.

Rule 67.   Blease v. Garlington, 92 U. S., 1.

LXXXII. If neither party requires the testimony to be taken orally in the method just described, then the same may be taken by depositions, according to the provisions of rule 67, or according to the acts of congress, or statutes of the state wherein the case is pending.

Rules 67, 68.   Revised Statutes, sections 863–875; 27 Statutes at Large, 7.

LXXXIII. If taken under the provisions of rule 67, the interrogatories must be written out and filed with the clerk, with a request to the clerk to issue a commission at the proper time, unless the parties agree that the testimony may be taken on oral interrogatories. Ten days' notice thereof must be given to the adverse party or his counsel, in order that cross-interrogatories may be filed.

The court or a judge thereof, or the clerk, if so authorized by general order, selects the person to act as commissioner, and upon the expiration of the ten days' notice issues to the party selected a commission, having attached thereto the interrogatories and cross-interrogatories to be propounded to the witness.

If testimony is taken upon written interrogatories the last interrogatory must be substantially in the following form:

"Do you know, or can you set forth, any other matter or thing which may be a benefit or advantage to the parties at issue in this cause, or either of them, or that may be material to the subject of this your examination, or the matter in question in this cause?

"If yea, set forth the same fully and at large in your answer."

Rules 67-71.

LXXXIV. Sections 863, 864 and 865 of the Revised Statutes contain the provisions authorizing taking depositions *de bene esse*.

According to section 863, if a witness lives at a greater distance than one hundred miles from the place of trial, or is bound on a sea voyage, or is about to go out of the United States, or out of the district in which the case is pending, and to a distance greater than one hundred miles from place of trial, or when he is ancient or infirm, the party wishing his evidence may take his deposition before any judge or clerk of a United States court, or before a commissioner of a circuit court, or before any judge of a state court, or before a mayor or chief magistrate of a city, or before a notary public, provided such party is not of counsel or an attorney for either party to the litigation, and is not interested in the event of the cause.

Reasonable written notice of the time, place and officer before whom the deposition is to be taken, with the names of the witnesses, must be given to the opposite party or his counsel.

Section 866 of the Revised Statutes provides that where it is necessary in order to prevent a failure or delay of justice, the court may grant a *dedimus potestatem* to take depositions according to common usage. And by the act of March 9, 1892, it is enacted that it shall be lawful to take the testimony or depositions of witnesses in the mode prescribed by the law of the state wherein the federal court is held.

27 Statutes at Large, 7.

LXXXV. If, after a bill is filed, and before the defendant has answered the same, it is made to appear by affidavit that any of the complainant's witnesses are aged and infirm, or are about to leave the country, or that any of them is a single witness to a material fact, the complainant may upon application procure from the clerk the issuance of a commission to such person as a judge of the court shall direct, to take the testimony of such witness or witnesses, due notice of the time and place of taking the same being given to the adverse party.

Rule 70.

LXXXVI. The court may, if it deems it advisable, permit witnesses to be examined *viva voce*, in open court.

If the case is appealable, the testimony thus heard should be taken down and made part of the record, or it will be disregarded by the appellate court.

Rules 67-78.   Blease v. Garlington, 92 U. S., 1.

LXXXVII. The circuit courts may appoint standing masters in chancery, and they may also appoint a master to act in a particular case.

Rule 82.

LXXXVIII. A master in chancery is an officer appointed by the court to assist it in various proceedings incidental to the progress of a cause before it, and is usually employed to take and state accounts, to take and report testimony, and to perform such duties as require computation of interest, the value of annuities, the amount of damages in particular cases, the auditing and ascertaining of liens upon property involved, and similar services.

Kimberly v. Arms, 129 U. S., 512.

LXXXIX. The court cannot, without the consent of the adversary parties, refer the decision of the entire case to a master, but with the consent of the parties such a reference may be made, and the findings of the master in such case will be taken to be presumptively correct and are not subject to be set

5

aside and disregarded at the mere discretion of the court.

Kimberly v. Arms, 129 U. S., 512; Davis v. Schwartz, 155 U. S., 631.

XC. The court on its motion, or at the request of either of the parties, may refer to a master any special matter arising in a case. Ordinarily, if after a hearing and decision by the court upon the pleadings or upon the pleadings and proofs of the main issues involved, it becomes necessary to have an examination and statement of accounts, or to ascertain the damages to be awarded, or to take further evidence in order to properly apply the rulings of the court to the facts of the case, a reference will be made.

The report of the master, upon a reference of this character, is merely advisory to the court, which may accept and act upon it, or may disregard it in whole or in part, according to its own judgment as to the weight of the evidence, although the conclusions of the master in weighing conflicting testimony have every reasonable presumption in their favor and will not be set aside unless error or mistake clearly appears.

Kimberly v. Arms, 129 U. S., 512; Tilghman v. Proctor, 125 U. S., 149; Callaghan v. Myers, 128 U. S., 617.

XCI. When a reference to a master is had, the party at whose instance the reference was had, or, if made by the court of its own motion, then the party upon whom the burden of proof lies, must, on or before the next rule day, bring the matter before the master, or, if he does not so do, the other party may bring the matter before the master at the costs of the delinquent party.

The matter is brought before the master by furnishing him a certified copy of the order of reference, and a request that he assign the time and place of proceeding with the hearing.

Rule 74.

XCII. The order of reference to a master should always clearly show what issue or matter is thus referred to him, whether the issues at large or only some special matter or matters connected therewith.

XCIII. The master assigns the time and place for the hearing, giving due notice thereof to the parties in interest or their solicitors.

If either party fails to appear at the proper time and place, after due notice thereof has been given, the master may proceed *ex parte,* or may adjourn to a future day, giving notice thereof to the absent party or his solicitor. It is the duty of the master to proceed with all reasonable diligence, and either party may, when cause exists, apply to the court or judge for an order to speed the proceedings.

Rule 75.

XCIV. The master has the power to regulate the proceedings before him; to direct the manner in which the matters shall be proven before him; to examine the parties and their witnesses either *viva voce*, or when necessary to cause depositions to be taken; to require the production of all books, papers, writings, vouchers and other documents applicable to the matters covered by the reference; and generally to do all other acts and direct all other inquiries and proceedings by him deemed necessary to fully and justly perform the duties imposed upon him.

   Rules 77-79. Story v. Livingston, 13 Pet., 359.

XCV. All affidavits, depositions and documents previously made, read or used in the court in the progress of the cause may be used before the master.[1]

When necessary the master may direct the taking of testimony to be used before him by depositions, the same to be taken according to the provisions of the acts of congress, or the master may issue a certificate to the clerk directing him to issue a commission for the examination of the named witnesses.[2]

If either party requires it, the testimony of witnesses examined *viva voce* before the master must be taken down by the master, or by some one appointed by him and in his presence, in order that the same may be preserved for use before the court.[3]

[1] Rule 80.
[2] Rule 77.
[3] Rule 81. Blease v. Garlington, 92 U. S., 1.

XCVI. Upon the completion of the hearing before the master his report is prepared, and, with the evidence taken before the master, is returned into the clerk's office, the date of such return being entered by the clerk in the order book.[1]

If either party desires to except to the report, the exceptions must be filed in the clerk's office within one month after the filing of the report.[2]

· The exceptions should clearly and specifically point out the matter or matters excepted to, so that upon the face thereof the court can see the grounds of exception, and the parts of the report excepted to.[3]

If no exceptions are filed within the month allowed, the report will stand confirmed upon the rule day next succeeding the expiration of the month allowed for filing exceptions.

If exceptions are filed they stand for hearing before the court, if then in session, and if not, then at the next session thereof.[2]

[1] Rules 76, 82, 83.
[2] Rule 83.
[3] Story v. Livingston, 13 Pet., 359; Foster v. Goddard, 1 Black, 506.

XCVII. When a case is at issue in such form as to require the taking of evidence, the parties should promptly determine whether the whole case is to be referred by consent to a master, in which event the mode of taking the evidence will be directed by the master, or whether the issues are to be submitted in the first instance to the court. If the latter course is pursued, then if it is desired that the testimony, or any part thereof, shall be taken *viva voce* before the court, an application for an order to that effect should be made to the court, for, unless the court permits, the testimony cannot be taken in this manner.

If it is desired that the witnesses be examined orally, but not in open court, then the requisite notice must be given to the opposite party and the services of an examiner must be secured.

If neither of these methods is adopted, then the testimony of the witnesses must be taken by deposition, and the documentary evidence not introduced in connection with the testimony of the witnesses should be filed with the clerk.

CHAPTER X.

WITNESSES — ATTENDANCE — MODES OF SUMMONING AND ENFORCING ATTENDANCE — FEES.

XCVIII. Witnesses living within the district wherein the cause is pending may be summoned to testify before the court, before a commissioner or examiner appointed to take testimony, or before a master to whom a reference has been made.[1]

Witnesses living without the district at distances not exceeding one hundred miles from the place of trial may, in like manner, be summoned to appear and testify.[2]

Witnesses living outside the district wherein the cause is pending, and more than one hundred miles from the place of trial, cannot be compelled to attend in person.

In such cases, if they do not voluntarily appear in person, their testimony must be taken before a commissioner or examiner at a place sufficiently near their residence to compel their attendance by subpœna.

When testimony is sought to be taken under a *dedimus*, a witness cannot be required to go out of the county of his residence, nor to a distance greater than forty miles from his place of residence. Nor can he be deemed guilty of contempt for not obeying a subpœna, unless his fee for going and returning, and for one day's attendance, is paid or tendered him at the time the subpœna is served.³

¹ Rule 78.
² Revised Statutes, section 876.
³ Revised Statutes, section 870.

XCIX. For attendance before a court, commissioner, examiner or master, witnesses are entitled to a *per diem* of $1.50, and to mileage at the rate of five cents for each mile traveled in going from his place of residence to the place of hearing and returning.

Revised Statutes, section 848.

C. Subpœnas for summoning witnesses are issued by the clerk. Subpœnas signed and sealed by the clerk, but without the names of the witnesses being set forth, may be furnished by the clerk to the parties litigant and their solicitors, or to a commissioner, examiner or master, any one of whom can insert the names of the parties to be summoned.

Rule 78.

CI. A refusal to obey a subpœna properly issued and served upon a witness, requiring him to appear and testify before a commissioner, examiner or master, is a contempt of court. In such case the commissioner, examiner or master may certify the facts into the clerk's office, and thereupon the court or judge may order the issuance of an attachment against the party in default.

Rule 78.

CII. When a commission issues for the taking the testimony of a witness at any place within any district or territory of the United States, the clerk of any United States court for such district or territory, upon the application of either party to the suit, or his agent, may issue a subpœna commanding the witness to appear and testify before the commissioner named in the commission, at a time and place stated in such subpœna.

If the witness, after due service of the subpœna, refuses or neglects to appear, or, after appearing, wrongfully refuses to testify, the judge of the court from which the subpœna issued may enforce obedience to such process, or punish the disobedience thereof as a contempt of court.

Revised Statutes, section 868.

CIII. If the witness whose testimony is sought to be taken upon commission is found within the District of Columbia, then the application for a summons to the witness must be made to a justice of the supreme court of the District, and due proof be made to him that the testimony of the witness is material and that a commission has issued for taking the same.

Revised Statutes, section 871.

CIV. Upon the application of either party to a suit, a judge of any court of the United States in any district or territory may order the clerk of his court to issue a *subpœna duces tecum* requiring the witness therein named to appear and testify before the commissioner at the time and place named in the subpœna, and to bring with him and produce before said commissioner any paper, writing, instrument, book or document supposed to be in his possession, the same to be described in said subpœna; provided it is made to appear to said judge, by affidavit or otherwise, that there is reason to believe that said writing, paper, instrument, book or document is in the possession or power of said witness, and if produced would be competent evidence on behalf of the party applying for the order.

For failure to obey such subpœna the party may be proceeded against for contempt before the judge granting said order.

Revised Statutes, section 869.

CHAPTER XI.

AMENDMENTS — SUPPLEMENTAL AND REVIVAL BILLS.

CV. The complainant is entitled, as a matter of course and without payment of costs, to amend the bill in any particular before a copy thereof has been taken by, or furnished to, a defendant; and, after copy taken, may amend as to matters of form, clerical errors, misnomer of parties, misdescription of premises, errors of date or failure to fill blanks.

If, after a copy of the bill has been taken by a defendant, but before a demurrer, plea or answer has been filed, the complainant desires to amend the bill in a material point, which he may do, he must furnish a copy of the amendment, or of the bill as amended, to the defendant, and pay defendant the costs occasioned thereby.

After a demurrer, plea or answer has been filed to the bill, but before a replication has been filed, the complainant may, upon motion or petition to a judge, without notice thereof to defendant, obtain an order allowing him to amend his bill on or before the next succeeding rule day.

After replication has been filed, complainant cannot withdraw the replication and file an amendment to the bill, except upon an order to that effect being granted by a judge, upon a motion or petition, with due notice of the application to the defendant, the motion or petition to be supported by an affidavit showing that the same is not made for delay or vexation, and that the amendment is material and could not have been sooner introduced into the bill.

If the complainant, having obtained leave to amend, does not file the same by the next succeeding rule day or the time specially named in the order, he will be deemed to have abandoned the same, and the cause must proceed as if no such application had been made.

Rules 28, 29.

CVI. Generally, defects in the form of the bill, in the non-joinder or misjoinder of parties, in the statement of improper matter, in the omission to state some material or pertinent matter, are matters to be remedied by filing an amendment; and also if, to meet the averments of the answer, it becomes necessary to set forth matters existing when the bill was filed, but which are not contained in the original bill, the same should be set forth by way of amendment.

So, also, leave to amend the bill at the hearing may be granted in furtherance of justice, if the proofs show that complainant is entitled to relief, but there appears need of the addition of a party, or of more precise averments of facts, or of an amendment of the prayer.

Revised Statutes, section 954. Neale v. Neale, 9 Wall., 1; The Tremolo Patent, 23 Wall., 518; Hardin v. Boyd, 113 U. S., 756; Graffam v. Burgess, 117 U. S., 180; Richmond v. Irons, 121 U. S., 27; Chicago, etc., Ry. Co. v. Chicago Nat. Bank, 134 U. S., 276; Gormley v. Bunyan, 138 U. S., 623.

CVII. The answer may be amended as a matter of course in a matter of form or as to filling blanks, correcting dates, or by reference to a document or other small matter, and be resworn to, at any time before a replication thereto is filed or the cause is set down for hearing upon bill and answer.

After replication is filed or the cause is set down for hearing on bill and answer, no material amendment can be made, except upon leave granted by the court or judge, after due notice of the application therefor given to the complainant.

Rule 60.

CVIII. When a pending suit becomes defective by the happening of some event after the filing of the bill, affecting the interest of the parties or the subject-matter of the suit, or for any other reason it becomes apparent that some new party should be brought in or some new fact should be alleged, the defect may be cured by filing a supplemental bill.

Application for leave to file same should be made to a judge upon a rule day, notice being given to the adversary party.

If leave is granted and the supplemental bill is filed the defendant must demur, plead or answer to the same on the next succeeding rule day, unless some other time is assigned by the judge. If new parties are brought in, a subpœna must be issued and served on them.

Rule 57. Kennedy v. Bank, 8 How., 586; Shaw v. Bill, 95 U. S., 10.

CIX. In suits wherein there are two or more complainants or two or more defendants, and one or more of them dies, and the cause of action survives in the remaining complainants or against the remaining defendants, the suit is not thereby abated, but upon suggestion of the death of the party entered upon the record, the suit continues.

Revised Statutes, section 956.

CX. When either of the parties, complainant or defendant, dies before final decree, the executor or administrator of such deceased party may, in case the cause of action survives by law, prosecute or defend such suit as though originally a party thereto.

If the executor or administrator does not voluntarily make himself a party, the adversary party may sue out a *scire facias* from the office of the clerk of the court wherein the suit is pending, requiring him to become a party or show cause to the contrary, and if he does not, within twenty days from service thereof, make himself a party or show sufficient cause, the court may render judgment against the estate of the deceased party the same as though the administrator or executor had voluntarily made himself a party.

Revised Statutes, section 955.

CXI. If, after the filing the bill and service of process, or waiver of same by entering an appearance, an event happens of such a nature as to abate the suit as then pending, as, for instance, the death of either party, then the suit, where the cause of action survives, may be revived by the filing of a bill of revivor, or a bill in the nature of a bill of revivor, as the circumstances may require.

The former lies in cases wherein the interest of the deceased party passes to another by reason of mere privity of blood or of representation by operation of law; the latter in cases wherein the interest of the deceased party passes to another by virtue of the act of the deceased. Thus, an heir may be made a party by a bill of revivor because he inherits by operation of law and as a privy by blood. An executor or administrator may also be made a party by a bill of revivor because they represent the deceased by operation of law.

In case, however, lands are devised to another by the deceased party, the devisee is brought in by a bill in the nature of a bill of revivor.

Practically the difference between the named forms of bills is reduced to the title thereof, as all that is essential therein is to set forth the title of the cause, aver its pendency in the court, the happening of the event abating the suit, and the name or names of the parties in whose favor or against whom it is sought to revive the suit, with a statement showing that they are the now proper parties, and praying that they may be made parties and for process against them. Upon the filing of the bill the clerk issues a subpœna requiring the proper representatives of the other party to appear and show cause why the suit should not be revived.

If cause is not shown at the rule day occurring next after fourteen days from service of the subpœna, the suit stands revived as matter of course.

If cause is shown, then the matter must be submitted for decision to the court or a judge thereof.

<small>Rule 56. Clarke v. Matthewson, 12 Pet., 164.</small>

CXII. The revival of a cause is not deemed to be the beginning of a new suit, but it is simply the continuance of the original proceeding.[1] The jurisdiction of the court is not affected nor defeated if the representative parties thus brought in are citizens of the same state with the adversary party.[1] Jurisdiction having once rightfully attached is not defeated by the subsequent changes in the parties necessitated by the abatement and revival of the suit.[1]

Evidence taken before the happening of the event necessitating the revival may be used in the further progress of the cause.[2]

<small>[1] Mollan v. Torrance, 9 Wheaton, 537; Clarke v. Matthewson, 12 Pet., 164.
[2] Vattier v. Hinde, 7 Pet., 252.</small>

CXIII. If a party to a final decree dies before an appeal is perfected within the time allowed for taking an appeal, and it is desired to take an appeal, it is not necessary to revive the suit by formal proceedings.

If the representative of such deceased party desires the appeal, he may file in the office of the clerk of the circuit court a duly certified copy of his appointment, and may thereupon enter an appeal as the party he represents might have done.

18 Statutes at Large, 473. Dolan v. Jennings, 139 U. S., 385.

CXIV. If the party in whose favor the decree was entered dies before appeal, and the other party desires to take the case to the supreme court, he may procure the allowance of an appeal, docket the case and file the record in the supreme court, suggest the death of the party, and in that court obtain an order that unless the representative of the deceased party appear and become a party within the first ten days of the ensuing term, the appellant shall have leave to open the record and submit the cause, a copy of such order being printed in some newspaper of general circulation within the state, territory or district from which the case is brought for three successive weeks, such publication to be completed at least sixty days before the beginning of the next term of the supreme court.

18 Statutes at Large, 473. Supreme Court Rules, No. 15.

CXV. In cases wherein the appeal lies to a circuit court of appeals and a party dies either before an appeal is taken or pending the hearing in the appellate court, the mode of procedure is governed by the following rules, which are the same in the several circuits:

1. Whenever pending a writ of error or appeal in this court, either party shall die, the proper representatives in the personalty or realty of the deceased

party, according to the nature of the case, may voluntarily come in and be admitted parties to the suit, and thereupon the case shall be heard and determined as in other cases; and if such representatives shall not voluntarily become parties, then the other party may suggest the death on the record, and thereupon, on motion, obtain an order that unless such representatives shall become parties within sixty days, the party moving for such order, if defendant in error, snall be entitled to have the writ of error or appeal dismissed, and, if the party so moving shall be plaintiff in error, he shall be entitled to open the record, and on hearing have the judgment or decree reversed, if it be erroneous: *Provided, however*, that a copy of every such order shall be personally served on said representatives at least thirty days before the expiration of such sixty days.

2. When the death of a party is suggested, and the representatives of the deceased do not appear within ten days after the expiration of such sixty days, and no measures are taken by the opposite party within that time to compel their appearance, the case shall abate.

3. When either party to a suit in a circuit or district court of the United States shall desire to prosecute a writ of error or appeal to this court from any final judgment or decree rendered in the circuit or district court, and at the time of suing out such writ of error or appeal the other party to the suit

shall be dead and have no proper representative within the jurisdiction of the court which rendered such final judgment or decree, so that the suit cannot be revived in that court, but shall have a proper representative in some state or territory of the United States, or in the District of Columbia, the party desiring such writ of error or appeal may procure the same, and may have proceedings on such judgment or decree superseded or stayed in the same manner as is now allowed by law in other cases, and shall thereupon proceed with such writ of error or appeal as in other cases. And within thirty days after the filing of the record in this court the plaintiff in error or appellant shall make a suggestion to the court, supported by affidavit, that the said party was dead when the writ of error or appeal was taken or sued out, and had no proper representative within the jurisdiction of the court which rendered such judgment or decree, so that the suit could not be revived in that court, and that said party had a proper representative in some state or territory of the United States, or in the District of Columbia, and stating therein the name and character of such representative, and the state or territory or district in which such representative resides; and upon such suggestion he may, on motion, obtain an order that, unless such representative shall make himself a party within ninety days, the plaintiff in error or appellant shall be entitled to open the record, and, on hearing, have the judgment or decree reversed if the same be erroneous: *Provided, however,* that a proper citation reciting the substance of such order shall be served upon such representative, either personally or by being left at his residence, at least thirty days before the expiration of such ninety days: *Provided, also,* that in every such case, if the representative of the deceased party does not appear within ten days after the expiration of such ninety days, and the measures above provided to compel the appearance of such representative have not been taken within the time as above required, by the opposite party, the case shall abate: *And provided, also,* that the said representative may at any time before or after said suggestion come in and be made a party to the suit, and thereupon the case shall proceed, and be heard and determined as in other cases.

CHAPTER XII.

PREPARATION FOR HEARING—SUBMISSION OF CAUSE—DECREE.

CXVI. Preparatory to submitting a cause to the court upon the pleadings and evidence, if the same are voluminous, proper abstracts thereof, with indexes thereto, should be prepared.

The evidence bearing upon each issue or distinct question of fact should, so far as possible, be grouped together.

There is no other step in the preparation and submission of a cause in which care, discrimination and thoroughness on part of counsel are of greater moment than in bringing together in logical and lucid form and sequence the vital issues in the case and the evidence applicable thereto.

CXVII. After the taking of the evidence is closed and before the final rendition of decree, if a party desires to present any new matter in the way of issue or evidence, he must apply for leave to the court or judge by petition setting up the new matter or issue, so that its relevancy and materiality can be judged of, and asking leave to introduce further evidence, or to amend the pleadings, and also showing the reasons why the party was not in fault in not earlier presenting the matter.

CXVIII. When the decision of the court is made known, a decree in accordance therewith should be prepared and be submitted to the judge for signature, and when signed must be filed with the clerk for entry.

In drawing up decrees no part of the pleadings, nor of the master's report or other prior proceedings, should be recited or stated in the decree.

It should, in apt terms, clearly set forth the exact conclusion and judgment of the court upon the issue or issues passed upon, and if by such judgment the defendant is required to abstain from doing any act, or is required to perform any act, the same should be set forth clearly, and, in case of performance required, the time, mode and conditions thereof should be made plain.

Rule 86.

CXIX. In suits for the foreclosure of mortgages, wherein the mortgaged property does not realize enough to pay the debt due complainant, a decree for the balance left unpaid may be rendered, and execution may issue therefor.

Rule 92.

CXX. After decree in the trial court, rehearings may be applied for by petition, although it is not necessary to ask for a new trial or rehearing in order to be entitled to take an appeal. Prior to the adoption of the act creating the circuit courts of appeals, an appeal could not be taken in all cases to the supreme court, and by Equity Rule 88 it was provided that in cases wherein an appeal could be taken to the supreme court, the petition for rehearing must be filed and brought to the attention of the court during the term at which the final decree was entered, but in cases wherein no appeal could be taken the trial court might permit the petition to be filed before the end of the term next after that at which the decree was entered. As an appeal in all cases either to the supreme court or a circuit court of appeals is now provided for, it would seem to follow that in all cases the application for a rehearing must be made during the term at which the final decree is entered.

The petition for rehearing must set forth clearly the special matter or cause on which the rehearing is sought, must be signed by counsel, and the facts relied on, if not already apparent on the record, must be verified by the oath of the party, or some other person having knowledge thereof. Notice of the application should be given to the adversary party or his solicitors. The granting or refusing a rehearing is a matter wholly within the discretion of the circuit court, and its action thereon cannot be appealed from.

Steines v. County, 14 Wall., 15; Buffington v. Harvey, 95 U. S., 99; Boesch v. Graff, 133 U. S., 697.

CXXI. In cases, therefore, in which it is desired to present to the circuit court grounds for a rehearing, and if the relief thus sought is refused, then to appeal from such refusal, the remedy must be sought by filing in the circuit court a bill of review.

If the error complained of is apparent upon the face of the record, by which is meant the bill, answer and other pleadings and proceedings, the master's report and the decree, but not including the evidence, then the same may be presented by a pure bill of review. In other words, upon a pure bill of review nothing can be urged as ground of reversal save error of law apparent on the face of the record.[1]

If, however, after decree rendered, discovery is made of any new matter of a nature sufficient to show error in the decree, or of new evidence material to the issue upon which the case was heard, and the party seeking the benefit thereof was not in fault in not discovering and presenting such matter or evidence before the hearing, relief by reason thereof may be sought by filing a bill of review, in which may be joined allegations showing error of law on the face of the record, as well as the allegations touching the newly-discovered matter or evidence.[2]

[1] Whiting v. Bank, 13 Pet., 6; Putnam v. Day, 22 Wall., 60; Buffington v. Harvey, 95 U. S., 99; Thompson v. Maxwell, 95 U. S., 391; Beard v. Burts, 95 U. S., 434; Clark v. Killian, 103 U. S., 766; Shelton v. Van Kleeck, 106 U. S., 532; Nickle v. Stewart, 111 U. S., 776; Bridge Co. v. Hatch, 125 U. S., 1.
[2] Buffington v. Harvey, 95 U. S., 99.

CXXII. Where a bill of review, based in whole or in part upon the alleged discovery of new matter or new evidence, is allowed and filed, it stands, so far as such new matter or evidence is concerned, as an original bill, to which the adversary party may interpose a demurrer or an answer. If, by reply to the answer, an issue of fact is made, evidence will be heard thereon, and if the facts alleged are found to be true, and to be sufficient to affect the original decree, the same will be opened, and, if necessary, a new hearing will be had, and the proper decree be entered.

If, upon demurrer or the hearing on the facts, it be held that the same are not sufficient to require a rehearing or the modification or reversal of the decree, the bill of review will be dismissed.

Upon such issue of fact the evidence adduced at the original hearing cannot be discussed for the purpose of showing error in the conclusions based thereon at the original hearing, although it may be adverted to for the purpose of showing the bearing and materiality of the new matter or evidence sought to be availed of by means of the bill of review.

Buffington v. Harvey, 95 U. S., 99; Craig v. Smith, 100 U. S., 226.

CXXIII. Bills of review based solely upon errors of law apparent on the face of the record are filable as matter of right, and ordinarily must be brought within the time limited by statute for taking an appeal.[1]

If a case is appealed and disposed of on its merits by the appellate court, then a bill of review, for errors appearing on the face of the record, cannot be entertained by the trial court, the remedy in such case being by a direct application to the appellate court.

Nor will a bill of review, on the ground of newly-discovered evidence, be entertained by the trial court after a decision on appeal, except by the permission or authority of the appellate court, evidenced by a reservation to that effect in the original decree ordered in the appellate court, or by an order granted upon an application to the appellate court for that purpose.[2]

[1] Whiting v. Bank, 13 Pet., 6; Thomas v. Harvie's Heirs, 10 Wheat., 146; Clark v. Killian, 103 U. S., 766; Ensminger v. Powers, 108 U. S., 292.

[2] Southard v. Russell, 16 How., 547; Ballard v. Searls, 130 U. S., 50; Kingsbury v. Buckner, 134 U. S., 650; In re Potts, 166 U. S., 263.

CXXIV. If, however, the cause is taken by appeal to an appellate court, but is not there heard upon the merits, but the appeal is dismissed without opportunity being had to present the merits, the party aggrieved may file a bill of review in the circuit court after the dismissal of the appeal, even though the time for an appeal may have elapsed, as in such case he could not file the bill while the appeal was pending, and under such circumstances the period during which the circuit court was deprived of jurisdiction is not computed in ascertaining whether the limitation has expired.[1]

When the bill is founded upon matters discovered since entry of decree, this limitation does not necessarily apply; yet as bills of this character are, ordinarily, appeals to the discretion of the chancellor, the matter of the lapse of time is always one of weight in deciding what equitable discretion demands in a given case.[2]

Hence a party against whom a decree has gone should be diligent in ascertaining whether cause for review exists, and upon discovery thereof should promptly apply for leave to file the proper bill.

Not only so, but he should, so far as it is in his power, perform the decree in all particulars, save those in which, by performance, he would defeat the rights sought to be protected by obtaining a review of the decree, and the reasons why the decree is not performed should be set forth in the bill.[3]

[1] Ensminger v. Powers, 108 U. S., 292.
[2] Thomas v. Harvie's Heirs, 10 Wheat., 146; Rubber Co. v. Goodyear, 9 Wall., 805; Ricker v. Powell, 100 U. S., 104.
[3] Ricker v. Powell, 100 U. S., 104; Davis v. Speiden, 104 U. S., 83.

CXXV. A bill of review is the proper remedy when it is sought to set aside a decree on the ground of fraud in the procurement thereof.

Tenny v. Bank, 92 U. S., 454.

CXXVI. The right to take an appeal, to petition for a rehearing, or to file a bill of review, is ordinarily confined to the parties appearing of record.

If, after the entry of a decree and before the appeal or rehearing is applied for, a party dies, his proper legal representative or the proper party succeeding to his interest should be made party on the record.

If one or more of a class represented on the record

by a few of the same class, or by a trustee or other like representative, desires an appeal or a rehearing for the protection of his interests, and he wishes to be heard in respect thereto, he should apply to the circuit court by petition and notice to the adversary party for leave to become a party to the record for the desired purpose.

Sage v. Railroad Co., 93 U. S., 412; Ex parte Cutting, 94 U. S., 14; Thompson v. Maxwell, 95 U. S., 391.

CHAPTER XIII.

PRELIMINARY INJUNCTIONS AND RESTRAINING ORDERS.

CXXVII. Pending the hearing and final disposition of cases in equity, writs of injunction, when cause therefor exists, may be issued by the circuit court or any judge thereof.

The justices of the supreme court cannot hear or allow any application for a restraining order or an injunction in a case pending in the circuit court, except within the limits of the judicial circuit to which they are severally assigned, except in cases wherein such application cannot be heard by the circuit or district judges.

As one of the judges of the circuit court, the district judge cannot order the issuance of an injunction, if the party applying therefor has had a reasonable time to apply to the circuit court for the writ.

An injunction allowed by a district judge continues in force only until the first day of the next term of the circuit court.

If it is desired to continue the same, an order to that effect must be procured from the court.

Revised Statutes, section 719. Parker v. Judges, 12 Wheaton, 561.

CXXVIII. When the bill prays an injunction to stay proceedings at law, if the defendant does not appear and plead, demur or answer to the same within the time required by the rules, the complainant is entitled as of course, and upon motion without notice, to the issuance of the writ for the purpose named.

In other cases injunctions are granted only after a hearing by the court if in session, or by a judge thereof, due notice of the application being first given to the adverse party.

Injunctions awarded in vacation, unless previously dissolved by the judge granting the same, continue in force until the next term of the court, or until dissolved by some order of court.

It is the safer practice, if it is desired to continue the injunction granted in vacation, to obtain an order for its continuance on the first day of the next ensuing term of the court.

Rule 55.

CXXIX. Upon notice being given of a motion for an injunction, the court or judge, if there appears to be danger of irreparable injury from delay, may grant an order restraining the act sought to be enjoined until the decision upon the motion for the injunction, which restraining order may be granted with or without security, in the discretion of the court or judge.

Revised Statutes, section 718.

CXXX. The courts of the United States, or the judges thereof, cannot by injunction stay proceedings in the courts of the state, except in cases where such injunction is authorized by the laws relating to proceedings in bankruptcy.

Revised Statutes, section 720.

CHAPTER XIV.

CROSS-BILLS.

CXXXI. A cross-bill, being a bill brought by a defendant against the complainant, or against other defendants, or against both, is usually filed (1) to obtain a discovery of facts in aid of the defense to the original bill, or (2) to obtain full relief touching the matters of the original bill.

When filed for the purposes of discovery only against the complainant, the defendant to the original bill must answer the original bill before the complainant therein can be required to answer the cross-bill.[1]

The statutory change in the admissibility of parties in interest as witnesses has largely obviated the necessity of resorting to a cross-bill for the sole purposes of discovery.

When filed for purposes of relief, the cross-bill must be based upon the matters in question in the original bill, and it must appear that a settlement of the controversy presented by the cross-bill is fairly necessary in order to enable the court to fully dispose of the litigation connected with the matter of the original bill.[2]

Leave to file a cross-bill must be procured before filing same or the bill may be disregarded at the hearing.[3]

New parties cannot be introduced by a cross-bill.[4]

The cross-bill should pray process against those made defendants thereto, and unless they appear to the cross-bill a subpœna should be issued and served upon them.[5]

The defendants therein may, by demurrer, plea or answer, make defense to the allegations and relief sought by the cross-bill.

[1] Rule 72.

[2] Cross v. De Valle, 1 Wall., 1; Rubber Co. v. Goodyear, 9 Wall., 807; Railroad Co. v. Chamberlain, 6 Wall., 748; Kingsbury v. Buckner, 134 U. S., 650; Chicago, etc., Ry. Co. v. Chicago Bank, 134 U. S., 276; Morgan Steamship Co. v. Texas Central R. R. Co., 137 U. S., 171.

[3] Bronson v. Railroad Co., 2 Wall., 283.

[4] Shields v. Barrow, 17 How., 130; Bank v. Railroad Co., 11 Wall., 624.

[5] Washington R. R. Co. v. Bradleys, 10 Wall., 299.

CHAPTER XV.

RIGHT OF INTERVENTION BY THIRD PARTIES.

CXXXII. Where a person not a party to the original bill has an interest by way of title, lien or otherwise in the property which forms the subject-matter of the suit, or which has, by means of process or order of the court, passed into the possession or under the control of the court, and such interest is liable to be affected by the proceedings, he may, by petition, apply to the court for leave to intervene for the protection of his rights, and such leave will be granted when cause exists.

The right of the court to grant such leave and to hear and adjudicate upon the rights of such intervener is not defeated by reason of the fact that such intervener and complainant are citizens of the same state.

If leave is granted, the party obtaining same must forthwith, unless time be granted, file his petition in the cause, setting forth his rights, and praying for the relief sought, and give notice of the filing thereof to the other parties to the cause.

Freeman v. Howe, 24 How., 450; Krippendorf v. Hyde, 110 U. S., 276; Gumbel v. Pitkin, 113 U. S., 545; Stewart v. Durham, 115 U. S., 61; Gumbel v. Pitkin, 124 U. S., 143.

CHAPTER XVI.

APPEALS TO SUPREME AND CIRCUIT COURT OF APPEALS.

CXXXIII. By section 1012 of the Revised Statutes it is enacted that appeals from the district and circuit courts shall be subject to the same rules, regulations and restrictions as are or may be prescribed in law in cases of writs of error, and hence it is that many sections of the statutes, which in terms refer only to writs of error, are held applicable also to cases on appeal.

Danville v. Brown, 128 U. S., 503.

CXXXIV. The adoption of the act of congress, approved March 3, 1891, creating the circuit courts of appeals, greatly changed and enlarged the right of appeal in equity cases. The appellate jurisdiction previously existing in the circuit courts is abolished; all previously existing limitations upon the right of appeal, based upon the amount in controversy, are swept away, and provision is made for an appeal in all cases cognizable in the district or circuit courts, the original appellate jurisdiction being distributed between the supreme court and the circuit courts of appeals within their respective circuits, provision being also made for securing ultimate uniformity of decision on all questions, by authorizing the several circuit courts of appeals to certify to the supreme court for its instruction specific questions of law arising in the cases pending before them, and by granting to the supreme court the power, by *certiorari* or otherwise, to cause to be brought before that court, for hearing and final decision, any case pending in a circuit court of appeals.

26 Statutes at Large, 826.   McLish v. Roff, 141 U. S., 661.

CXXXV. According to the provisions of the act of 1891, the appeal lies to the supreme court,—

When the jurisdiction of the trial court is in issue, in which case the question of jurisdiction alone is certifiable to the supreme court;

When the case involves the construction or application of the constitution of the United States;

When in the case there is drawn in question the constitutionality of any law of the United States, or the validity or construction of any treaty made under the authority of the United States;

When in the case it is claimed that the constitution or law of a state is in contravention of the constitution of the United States.[1]

In all other cases the appeal lies in the first instance from a final order or decree of the circuit court to the circuit court of appeals of the proper circuit.[1] And in cases wherein an appeal to a circuit court of appeals will lie from the final decree, an appeal to the proper circuit court of appeals may be taken from an interlocutory order or decree granting, continuing, refusing, dissolving or refusing to dissolve an injunction.[2]

[1] 26 Statutes at Large, 828.
[2] 28 Statutes at Large, 666.

CXXXVI. In construing the provisions of the statute regulating appeals, the supreme court has laid down the following rules for determining the court to which appeals are to be taken in the first instance:

If the jurisdiction of the circuit court is questioned and the decision of the trial court is against the existence of jurisdiction, thus resulting in the dismissal of the case, the party interested in sustaining the jurisdiction must have the question of jurisdiction properly certified and thereupon take an appeal to the supreme court.

If the jurisdiction of the circuit court, being questioned, is sustained, an appeal cannot be taken until the case is determined on the merits; and if upon the merits the decree is for the defendant, then the complainant must appeal the whole case to the proper circuit court of appeals, and if in that court the question of the jurisdiction of the trial court arises, the circuit court of appeals may certify it to the supreme court for decision.

If the jurisdiction of the circuit court, being questioned, is sustained, and upon the merits the decree is in favor of the complainant, the defendant may elect to stand upon the question of jurisdiction alone, in which event the appeal will be to the supreme court direct, or he may elect to carry the whole case by appeal to the proper circuit court of appeals, and if in that court the question of the jurisdiction of the circuit court is presented, it may be certified by the circuit court of appeals to the supreme court.

If the jurisdiction of the circuit court, being questioned, is sustained, and a decree on the merits is rendered against the defendant, yet touching which the complainant has ground of complaint, the latter may take an appeal on the merits to the proper circuit court of appeals. The defendant may take an appeal on the question of jurisdiction to the supreme court direct, or may appeal the case to a circuit court of appeals, but cannot do both. If the defendant appeals to the supreme court on the question of jurisdiction, the complainant can appeal to a circuit court of appeals on the merits, which court will entertain the appeal, but will suspend a decision on the merits until the supreme court has passed on the question of jurisdiction. If the defendant appeals to a circuit court of appeals on the merits, the complainant may take a cross-appeal to the same court, and if the question of jurisdiction is presented the circuit court of appeals may certify the same to the supreme court for decision; and the same rules apply to cases wherein the complainant questions the jurisdiction of the circuit court, but the jurisdiction is sustained and a decree is entered upon the merits with which the complainant is, or both complainant and defendant are, dissatisfied.

United States v. Jahn, 155 U. S., 109; Robinson v. Caldwell, 165 U. S., 359.

CXXXVII. From the rules thus established it follows that the one party cannot take an appeal to the supreme court upon the question of jurisdiction and also take an appeal to a circuit court of appeals on the merits; but one party may go by appeal to the supreme court on the question of the jurisdiction of the circuit court, and the adversary party may take an appeal on the merits to a circuit court of appeals.

McLish v. Roff, 141 U. S., 661; United States v. Jahn, 155 U. S., 109.

CXXXVIII. In cases wherein an appeal lies direct to the supreme court, on the ground that there is involved therein the construction or application of some provision of the constitution of the United States, or the constitutionality of a law of the United States, or the construction or validity of a treaty of the United States, or the validity of the constitution or law of a state, and a general appeal is allowed, the supreme court has the power to dispose of the entire case upon the merits, including the question of jurisdiction.

Chappell v. United States, 160 U. S., 499; Robinson v. Caldwell, 165 U. S., 359.

CXXXIX. Appellate jurisdiction may be exercised by the supreme court over cases pending in the circuit courts of appeals in three modes, to wit: By entertaining questions of law duly certified to it from a court of appeals; by issuing a writ of *certiorari* to a court of appeals and thereby causing the record in the case to be sent up to the supreme court for its consideration; by means of an appeal properly taken in cases wherein by statute an appeal is given as matter of right.

In section 6 of the act of March 3, 1891, creating the circuit courts of appeals, it is provided that in any case coming within the appellate jurisdiction of a circuit court of appeals that court may certify to the supreme court any questions or propositions of law concerning which it desires the instruction of the supreme court for the proper decision of the case pending before it. In form, the certificate of the questions to be submitted must be prefaced with a brief statement of the nature of the case, and with a proper statement of the facts, sufficient to show the pertinency of the questions of law upon which the instructions of the supreme court are sought.[1] The questions submitted must be of law only, and not of fact or of law and fact intermingled or combined, and must not present the entire case split up into questions of law.[2]

[1] Supreme Court Rule 37.
[2] Graves v. Faurot, 162 U. S., 435; Cross v. Evans, 167 U. S., 60; Warner v. New Orleans, 167 U. S., 467.

CXL. If, upon examination of questions of law thus certified from a circuit court of appeals, the supreme court deems it advisable, it may require that the whole record and cause be sent up to it from the circuit court of appeals, and may thereupon decide the whole matter in controversy in the same manner as if it had been brought there for review by an original appeal; and if application for that purpose is made to the supreme court, a certified copy of the record must accompany the application.

[1] 26 Statutes at Large, 828; Supreme Court Rule 37.

CXLI. It is furthermore provided in section 6 of the act of March 3, 1891, that in any case wherein an appeal does not exist as a matter of right to the supreme court from the decision of a court of appeals, the supreme court may require, by *certiorari* or otherwise, that the case be certified to it for its review and determination.

It is held that the power thus granted to the supreme court to require a case to be certified to it is one to be sparingly exercised and only in cases of peculiar gravity and importance, or where necessary to secure uniformity of decision in the several circuits.

<small>In re Lau Ow Bew, 141 U. S., 583; Lau Ow Bew v. United States, 144 U. S., 47; In re Woods, 143 U. S., 202; Amer. Const. Co. v. Railway Co., 148 U. S., 372; Forsyth v. Hammond, 166 U. S., 506.</small>

CXLII. When the issuance of a *certiorari* is sought under this clause of the statute, the petition therefor must be filed in the supreme court, must contain a clear statement of the grounds relied upon for the issuance of the writ, and must be accompanied with a certified copy of the entire record of the case, as the same exists in the circuit court of appeals.

<small>Supreme Court Rule 37.</small>

CXLIII. By the provisions of section 6 of the act of March 3, 1891, the decisions of the circuit courts of appeal are made final in all cases wherein the federal jurisdiction is dependent entirely upon the opposite parties to the suit or controversy being aliens and citizens of the United States or citizens of different states, and in cases arising under the patent or revenue laws. In all other cases determinable in a circuit court of appeals, a right of appeal to the supreme court exists from the decision of the circuit court of appeals, provided the matter in controversy exceeds in amount the sum of $1,000, exclusive of costs.

The mode of taking such appeal is the same as in cases of appeal from a circuit court, requiring the filing of an assignment of errors in the circuit court of appeals, the allowance of an appeal by a judge of that court or by a justice of the supreme court and the filing of the transcript in the supreme court, the time limited for taking an appeal in such cases being one year.

CXLIV. To authorize an appeal under this clause of the act, it must appear that the matter actually in controversy exceeds in value the sum of $1,000 besides costs, and therefore, unless upon the face of the record this value is made to appear, evidence thereof should be supplied by affidavits; and the better practice is to file them in the trial court and to obtain a finding of that court upon the question of the amount involved,[1] although such finding is not binding on the supreme court.[2]

It is the amount involved in the controversy, when sought to be appealed, that determines the jurisdiction. Thus, if a party seeks to recover money or property in excess of $1,000 and recovers a part, he cannot appeal unless the difference between the recovery and the amount or value of the property he sought to recover exceeds $1,000.[2]

[1] Wilson v. Blair, 119 U. S., 387; Red River Cattle Co. v. Needham, 137 U. S., 632; Rector v. Lipscomb, 141 U. S., 557.

[2] Hilton v. Dickinson, 108 U. S., 165; New England Mortgage Co. v. Gay, 145 U. S., 123; Hollander v. Fechheimer, 162 U. S., 326.

CXLV. In cases wherein the decision and decree of a circuit court of appeals are made final under the sixth section of the act of March 3, 1891, and wherein orders or decrees are rendered upon proceedings in intervention or in auxiliary or ancillary proceedings, an appeal to the supreme court cannot be taken from a circuit court of appeals with respect thereto, as decrees entered in accessory and subordinate proceedings partake of the nature of the decree in the original suit.

Rouse v. Letcher, 156 U. S., 47; Gregory v. Van Ee, 160 U. S., 643; Carey v. Houston & Texas Ry. Co., 161 U. S., 115.

CHAPTER XVII.

TIME WITHIN WHICH APPEALS CAN BE TAKEN.

CXLVI In cases appealable in the first instance to the supreme court, the appeal must be taken within two years from the entry of the order or decree appealed from, unless the party seeking the appeal is an infant, insane, or imprisoned, in which cases the time during which such disability exists is excluded from computation.

Revised Statutes, section 1008.

CXLVII. In cases appealable in the first instance to a circuit court of appeals, the appeal must be taken within six months after the entry of the order or decree sought to be reviewed,[1] unless a shorter time is allowed by the act creating the right of appeal,[2] as in cases of appeal from an order granting, continuing, refusing, dissolving or refusing to dissolve a writ of injunction, in which cases the appeal must be taken in thirty days.

[1] 26 Statutes at Large, 829.
[2] 28 Statutes at Large, 666.

CXLVIII. In cases appealable, as matter of right, from the circuit courts of appeals to the supreme court, the appeal must be taken within one year from the entry of the order or decree by the circuit court of appeals.

26 Statutes at Large, 828.

CXLIX. In cases wherein an appeal is sought to a circuit court of appeals from an interlocutory order or decree granting, continuing, refusing, dissolving or refusing to dissolve an injunction, the appeal must be taken within thirty days from the entry of the order or decree.

28 Statutes at Large, 666.

CL. In computing the time within which an appeal may be taken, the day on which the order or decree sought to be appealed from was entered is not included.[1]

If an application for a rehearing is duly filed in and entertained by the trial court, the time limited for taking an appeal does not begin to run until the application for rehearing is overruled.[2]

[1] Smith v. Gale, 137 U. S., 577.
[2] Brocket v. Brocket, 2 How., 238; Memphis v. Brown, 94 U. S., 715; Texas & Pacific Ry. Co. v. Murphy, 111 U. S., 488; Aspen Mining Co. v. Billings, 150 U. S., 31.

CLI. If upon the entry of an order or decree an appeal therefrom is allowed, the trial court during the term at which the decree is entered, and before the jurisdiction of the appellate court attaches by the filing of the transcript in that court, may entertain an application for a rehearing, and if the same is granted the jurisdiction of the trial court remains unaffected, and the appeal cannot be perfected.[1]

If in such case the application for rehearing is entertained, but upon consideration is refused, then a new appeal should be taken, the same as though an appeal had not been previously allowed, as it is the overruling of the application for a rehearing which renders the decree final and therefore appealable.[2]

[1] Goddard v. Ordway, 101 U. S., 745; Keyser v. Farr, 105 U. S., 265; Aspen Mining Co. v. Billings, 150 U. S., 31.

[2] Voorhees v. Noye Man. Co., 151 U. S., 135.

CLII. If the last day of the period fixed by statute for taking an appeal falls upon a non-juridical day, such as Sunday or a legal holiday, the time for taking an appeal ends with the day preceding the non-juridical day. This is the rule held by the circuit court of appeals in the eighth circuit in the case of Johnson v. Myers, 4 C. C. A., 399; and although as stated by the supreme court in Street v. United States, 133 U. S., 299, the general rule is that a power that may be exercised up to and including a given day, if that day falls on Sunday, may be exercised on the following day, yet, in cases of appeal, safety lies in taking the appeal within the time limited, according to the ruling in Johnson v. Myers, *supra*.

CHAPTER XVIII.

ALLOWANCE OF APPEALS — CITATION — RETURN DAY — ASSIGNMENT OF ERRORS — SECURITY — SUPERSEDEAS.

CLIII. During the term at which the order or decree sought to be appealed from was entered, the appeal may be allowed in open court without filing a petition to that end; but, unless thus allowed in open court, a petition praying an appeal must be prepared, and be submitted to a judge or justice authorized to grant an appeal in the particular case. Under the rules now in force, an assignment of errors must be filed with the clerk of the circuit court before an appeal is properly allowable.

Brown v. McConnell, 124 U. S., 489.

CLIV. If an appeal allowed in open court is perfected by filing in the appellate court the transcript and docketing the case within the required time, the issuance and service of a citation is not necessary; but, unless the case is properly docketed and in cases wherein an appeal is allowed upon petition and not in open court, a citation must be issued and be served within the time fixed by the rules of the appellate court, or the appeal will become inoperative.

Hewitt v. Filbert, 116 U. S., 142; Jacobs v. George, 150 U. S., 415.

CLV. A citation is a notice admonishing the adversary party that an appeal in the given case has been allowed, and that he must appear at the proper time in the appellate court if he wishes to be heard in the cause, and is signed by a judge or justice authorized to grant an appeal in the particular case.

CLVI. In cases appealed to the supreme court the citation must be made returnable not exceeding thirty days from its date, whether the return day fall in vacation or in term time, and must be served before the return day, except in appeals from California, Oregon, Nevada, Washington, New Mexico, Utah, Arizona, Montana, Wyoming, North Dakota, South Dakota, Alaska and Idaho, in which cases the time is extended to sixty days.

Supreme Court Rules 8, 9.

CLVII. In cases appealed from final orders and decrees to the circuit courts of appeal, the citation must be made returnable not exceeding thirty days from its date, whether the return day fall in vacation or in term time, and must be served before the return day, except in the eighth circuit, wherein the time is sixty days, and except also in the fifth circuit, in cases of appeal from an order granting, continuing, dissolving or refusing to dissolve an injunction under the provisions of the act of February 18, 1895, wherein the citation must be made returnable and be served within ten days from its date.

Circuit Courts of Appeal Rules, 14.

CLVIII. As already stated, the party desiring to take an appeal must file with the clerk of the trial court a proper assignment of errors, and an appeal is not properly allowable until the assignment is filed. If allowed without the filing of an assignment of error, the appellate court may dismiss the appeal, although it may notice a plain error appearing on the record.

Revised Statutes, section 997; Supreme Court Rule 35; Circuit Courts of Appeals Rules 11. Churchill v. Farrar, 135 U. S., 609.

CLIX. The assignment should set out separately and particularly each error intended to be urged before the appellate court, and in case the error alleged is to the admission or rejection of evidence, the assignment must quote the full substance of the evidence admitted or rejected.

The purpose of the assignment of errors is to point out to the appellate court, and to the appellee, the specific questions which are to be submitted for decision, and each error assigned should include but one question only, stated with fullness sufficient so that the gist thereof can be gathered from the assignment itself.

On the one hand, therefore, it is necessary that the errors assigned should be sufficient in number and be sufficiently specific to fairly cover and point out the several matters in which it is claimed the trial court erred, and this is not accomplished by errors assigned in general terms. And on the other hand, it is advisable to avoid assigning a large number of errors, covering every possible detail in which it might be claimed error existed, or repeating the same question in slightly varying forms.

The aim should be to reduce the errors assigned to the number necessary to fairly present the questions at issue, and then to make each specification of error sufficiently full and clear so that no doubt will exist touching the question intended to be presented thereby.

CLX. The record must show that the questions upon which errors are assigned were raised in the trial court, as the assignment of errors cannot be availed of as a means for importing into the case questions not presented to the trial court.

Ansbro v. United States, 159 U. S., 695.

CLXI. The petition praying an appeal to the supreme court from an order or decree of a district or circuit court may be submitted for allowance to and be allowed by any district judge within his district, by any circuit judge within his circuit, or by any justice of the supreme court.

CLXII. If the appeal is sought to the circuit court of appeals from an order or decree of a district or circuit court, the petition may be submitted to and allowed by any district judge in cases pending within his district, by any circuit judge in cases pending within his circuit, and by the supreme justice assigned to the circuit wherein the case is pending.

CLXIII. If the appeal is sought from a judgment or decree of a circuit court of appeals to the supreme court, the petition for allowance may be submitted to and allowed by any of the judges of the court of appeals from which the appeal is sought, or by any of the justices of the supreme court.

CLXIV. The judge by whom an appeal is allowed will designate the amount of the bond required as a condition of appeal.

If it is desired to supersede the execution of the order or decree appealed from, the bond must be conditioned that the appellant shall prosecute his appeal to effect and answer all damages and costs if he fail to make his plea good; and the amount thereof, where the decree is for the recovery of money not otherwise secured, must be in a sum sufficient to cover the whole amount of the judgment, including just damages for delay and costs and interest on the appeal; but where the property in controversy necessarily follows the suit, as in real actions and mortgage foreclosures, or where the property or its proceeds or a bond for its value is in the hands of the marshal or in possession of the court, the amount of the bond need be only in a sum sufficient to secure the sum recovered for the use and detention of the property, the costs of suit, and just damages for delay and costs and interest on appeal.

Revised Statutes, section 1000; Supreme Court Rule 29; Circuit Courts of Appeals Rule 13.

CLXV. If the appeal is not to act as a *supersedeas*, then the bond is conditioned that the appellant shall prosecute his appeal to effect, and if he fail to make good his plea shall answer all costs.

In cases brought up by the United States or by direction of any department of the government, no security is required to be given.

The judge or justice who allows the appeal or signs the citation, or one who is authorized so to do, must approve the security, and this duty cannot be delegated to the clerk.

Revised Statutes, section 1000; O'Reilly v. Edgington, 96 U. S., 724.

CLXVI. On appeals from interlocutory orders or decrees granting, continuing, dissolving or refusing to dissolve injunctions, the court may at its discretion require the filing of an additional injunction bond, and the appellant must also file a bond as security for costs.

28 Statutes at Large, 666.

CLXVII. In cases wherein the appellant desires to stay the execution of an order or decree pending an appeal therefrom, he must procure the allowance of an appeal and give the required security, duly approved, within sixty days, Sundays not included, after the entry of the order or decree.

If the appeal is allowed within the sixty days, but the requisite security is not given and approved within that time, the same, by permission of a justice or judge of the appellate court, may be afterwards given, and process on the decree be stayed.

Revised Statutes, sections 1007–1012; 18 Statutes at Large, 318. Telegraph Co. v. Eyser, 19 Wall., 419.

CLXVIII. A *supersedeas* of its own force does not suspend the effect of a final decree granting, refusing or dissolving an injunction. To accomplish this, a justice or judge who took part in the decision of the cause may in his discretion, at the time of the allowance of the appeal, make an order suspending or modifying the injunction pending the appeal, upon such terms as to bond and otherwise as he may deem proper for the security of the rights of the opposite party.

Rule 93. Hovey v. McDonald, 109 U. S., 150; Knox v. Harshman, 132 U. S., 14.

CHAPTER XIX.

APPEALABLE DECREES — FINAL — INTERLOCUTORY.

CLXIX. Except in the case of appeals from orders with respect to injunctions, an appeal can be taken only from final orders or decrees.[1] Ordinarily an appeal will not lie until all the matters in controversy between the parties to the record have been determined, so as to obviate the necessity of successive appeals.[2]

If, however, the suit involves separable matters of controversy and the trial court determines them separately, an appeal may be taken from each decree entered, which is final with respect to the controversy affected by it.[3]

[1] Revised Statutes, section 692. Mordecai v. Lindsay, 19 How., 199.
[2] Forgay v. Conrad, 6 How., 200.
[3] Hill v. Chicago, etc., R. R. Co., 140 U. S., 52; Rouse v. Letcher, 156 U. S., 47.

CLXX. Successive appeals may be taken in cases wherein the court enters a decree final in its effect upon the matters in litigation, and therefore appealable, and subsequently enters orders or decrees in execution of the prior decree. The second or successive appeals are available only for the purpose of correcting errors in the subsequent decrees.

Railroad Co. v. Fosdick, 106 U. S., 47; Lewisburg Bank v. Sheffey, 140 U. S., 445; Hill v. Railroad Co., 140 U. S., 52.

CLXXI. If the decree accomplishes the purposes of the suit by determining the litigated matters or the questions included within the issues, and, without further judicial action, fixes the rights and liabilities of the parties, as by settling the title or right of possession to property, or directing the performance of a specific act, or directing the sale of property upon foreclosure of mortgages or other liens, in these and like cases the decree is deemed to be final for the purposes of appeal, although the trial court may continue its jurisdiction over the case for ministerial purposes, such as making sale of property or taking an account rendered necessary by the terms of the decree, or otherwise executing the decree rendered.

Decrees held final: Ray v. Law, 3 Cranch, 179; Whiting v. Bank, 13 Peters, 6; Forgay v. Conrad, 6 How., 201; Wabash v. Beers, 1 Black, 54; Bronson v. Railroad Co., 2 Black, 524; Blossom v. Railroad Co., 1 Wall., 655; Thomson v. Dean, 7 Wall., 342; Railroad Co. v. Bradley, 7 Wall., 575; French v. Shoemaker, 12 Wall., 86; Crosby v. Buchanan, 23 Wall., 420; Fuller v. Claflin, 93 U. S., 14; Ex parte Railroad Co., 95 U. S., 221; Winthrop v. Meeker, 109 U. S., 180; First National Bank v. Shedd, 121 U. S., 74; Stewart v. Masterson, 131 U. S., 151; In re Farmers' Loan & Trust Co., 129 U. S., 206; Central Trust Co. v. Grant Locomotive Works, 135 U. S., 207; Wheeling & B. Bridge Co. v. Wheeling Bridge Co., 138 U. S., 287; Fowler v. Hamill, 139 U. S., 549; Hill v. Chicago R. R. Co., 140 U. S., 52; Bank v. Sheffey, 140 U. S., 445.

CLXXII. If, however, the decree, although in form final, cannot be immediately carried into effect, and does not execute itself, but to that end needs further judicial action on part of the court, it is deemed to be interlocutory only, and therefore an appeal cannot be taken therefrom.

Decrees held not final: Hiriart v. Ballou, 9 Peters, 156; Lea v. Kelly, 15 Peters, 213; Young v. Smith, 15 Peters, 287; Perkins v. Fourniquet, 6 How., 206; Pulliam v. Christian, 6 How., 209; Craighead v. Wilson, 18 How., 199; Beebe v. Russel, 19 How., 283; Ogilvie v. Knox Ins. Co., 2 Black, 539; Humiston v. Stainthorpe, 2 Wall., 106; Wheeler v. Harris, 13 Wall., 51; Thomas v. Woolbridge, 23 Wall., 283; Railroad Co. v. Swasey, 23 Wall., 405; Butterfield v. Usher, 91 U. S., 246; Bostwick v. Brinkerhoff, 106 U. S., 3; Grant v. Insurance Co., 106 U. S., 429; Grant v. Insurance Co., 121 U. S., 118; Bank v. Whitney, 121 U. S., 284; Parsons v. Bostwick, 122 U. S., 112; Railroad Co. v. Simmons, 123 U. S., 52; Barker v. Craig, 127 U. S., 213; Keystone Manganese Co. v. Martin, 132 U. S., 91; Winters v. Ettrell, 132 U. S., 207; Meagher v. Thresher Co., 145 U. S., 608; McGourkey v. Toledo & O. C. R. Co., 146 U. S., 536; Luxton v. North River Bridge Co., 147 U. S., 337; Hohorst v. Hamburg Am. Packet Co., 148 U. S., 262; Latta v. Kilbourn, 150 U. S., 524.

CLXXIII. The general rule allowing appeals to be taken from final decrees only is qualified by the provisions of the act of congress approved February 18, 1895,[1] amending section 7 of the act approved March 3, 1891,[2] providing for an appeal to a circuit court of appeals from an interlocutory order or decree granting, continuing, refusing, dissolving or refusing to dissolve an injunction, in all cases wherein an appeal from a final decree will lie to a circuit court of appeals; and upon such an appeal, if the record before the appellate court is such that thereby the merits of the controversy are presented, the appellate court may decide the controversy on the merits, not being limited to the consideration of the order made with respect to the injunction.³

¹ 28 Statutes at Large, 666.
² 26 Statutes at Large, 828.
³ Smith v. Vulcan Iron Works, 165 U. S., 518.

CLXXIV. Previous to the adoption of the acts of congress just cited, it was held that in cases brought under the patent laws of the United States, to secure relief by way of injunction and an accounting for profits or damages, a decree sustaining the validity of the patent sued on, finding infringement thereof on part of the defendant and granting an injunction in restraint thereof, was not final for purposes of an appeal, if the trial court, by reference to a master or otherwise, continued to deal with the question of damages, that being one of the main issues presented by the bill filed in the case. But since the adoption of the acts of congress just cited, it is held that an appeal to the proper circuit court of appeals may be taken from the decree granting the injunction before the issue with regard to damages or profits is disposed of by the trial court. And from this it follows that upon an appeal in patent cases, whether from the granting, dissolving or refusing to grant a strictly preliminary injunction, or from the granting, continuing or refusing an injunction after hearing upon the merits, the appellate court, if the record filed therein presents the necessary facts, may determine the question whether the complainant has shown himself entitled to relief, and is not limited merely to a consideration of the propriety of granting, continuing, dissolving or refusing an injunction.

Smith v. Vulcan Iron Works, 165 U. S., 518.

CLXXV. By the terms of the acts of congress approved March 3, 1891, and February 18, 1895, the right of appeal therein provided for from interlocutory orders or decrees is limited to cases in which an appeal may be taken from a final decree to a circuit court of appeals, and the right of appeal thus provided for does not apply to cases wherein the original appeal must be taken to the supreme court.

CLXXVI. The general rule is that the whole cause or controversy, so far as possible, should be brought before the appellate court at the same time, and that all the parties united in interest and affected by the decree must join in the appeal. Therefore if the order or decree is joint and affects the interests of all, all should join in the appeal or it may be dismissed.

Owings v. Kincannon, 7 Peters, 399; Williams v. Bank of United States, 11 Wheat., 414; Simpson v. Greeley, 20 Wall., 152; Hanrick v. Patrick, 119 U. S., 156; Mason v. United States, 136 U. S., 581; Hardee v. Wilson, 146 U. S., 179; Beardsley v. Ark. & La. Ry. Co., 158 U. S., 123.

CLXXVII. If, however, one or more of the parties whose interests are affected by the order or decree refuse to join in taking an appeal, the remaining parties affected thereby can secure the right to an appeal by resorting to the process of summons and severance, or the equivalent thereof, which is accomplished by serving a written notice upon the party who refuses to join in the appeal that an appeal is about to be taken and inviting him to unite therein, and if he fails so to do, or does not appear in the trial court in response to the notice, that court can grant an appeal to the party asking it and bar the other parties from subsequently taking an appeal.

These proceedings should be made part of the record and be included in the transcript filed in the appellate court.

Todd v. Daniel, 16 Peters, 521; Masterson v. Herndon, 10 Wall., 416; Hardee v. Wilson, 146 U. S., 179; Inglehart v. Stansbury, 151 U. S., 68.

CLXXVIII. If the case is such that the order or decree affects only the interests of one or more of the parties to the record, leaving the interests of the remaining parties unaffected, then those whose interests are affected may appeal without joining the remaining parties therein.

Forgay v. Conrad, 6 How., 203; Germain v. Mason, 12 Wall., 261; Simpson v. Greeley, 20 Wall., 152; Gilfillan v. McKee, 159 U. S., 303.

CLXXIX. Even though one is a party to the record, he cannot take an appeal from an order or decree unless the same affects his interest.

Farmers' Loan & Trust Co. v. Waterman, 106 U. S., 265.

CLXXX. An appeal can be taken only by a party to the record.

Therefore, one whose interests are affected by a suit in equity, but who is not a party to the record, if he wishes to appeal from the decree therein, must apply to the trial court by petition and notice to the adversary party for leave to become a party to the record for the purpose of taking an appeal.

Sage v. Railroad Co., 93 U. S., 412; Ex parte Cutting, 94 U. S., 14.

CLXXXI. A purchaser of property sold under a decree rendered in a suit in equity has a right to be heard in the trial court upon all questions arising subsequent to the decree authorizing the sale which affect his bid or the burdens assumed by him as purchaser, and he has the right to appeal from orders or decrees affecting his rights as purchaser.

Kneeland v. American Loan Co., 136 U. S., 89.

CLXXXII. To perfect an appeal it is not only necessary that all jointly interested as appellants should join therein, unless a severance is allowed, but it is also necessary that all parties adversely interested should be made parties to the appeal by being duly notified of the appeal, which fact must be made apparent upon the record filed in the appellate court.

CLXXXIII. The appeal must be taken, both as to appellants and appellees, in the individual names of the parties, and not in the name of a firm or other collective designation.

This rule does not apply to corporations having authority to sue, and being liable to suit, in the corporate name.

Estes v. Trabue, 128 U. S., 225.

CLXXXIV. Decrees rendered by consent will not be reversed on the appeal of any of the consenting parties. An appeal may be taken therefrom, but the appellate court will affirm, without considering errors assigned thereon, all matters properly within the assent of the parties to the decree rendered.

Pacific R. R. Co. v. Ketchum, 101 U. S., 289; Nashville Ry. Co. v. United States, 113 U. S., 261.

CLXXXV. An appeal will not ordinarily lie from a decree upon the mere matter of costs, and especially when the question of costs is within the discretion of the trial court; and if an appeal be taken from a decree upon the merits and the same is affirmed with respect to the merits, it will not be reversed upon the question of costs.

Elastic Fabric Co. v. Smith, 100 U. S., 110; Paper Bag Machine Cases, 105 U. S., 766; Wood v. Weimar, 104 U. S., 786; Russell v. Farley, 105 U. S., 433; Trustees v. Grenough, 105 U. S., 527; Burns v. Rosenstein, 135 U. S., 449; Du Bois v. Kirk, 158 U. S., 58.

CLXXXVI. If, however, the decree awarding costs is attacked on the ground that the trial court had not jurisdiction over the case, and hence could not award costs,[1] or on the ground that costs were ordered paid from a fund not liable therefor,[2] or against a party not within the jurisdiction of the trial court,[3] or against whom liability for costs does not rightfully exist, an appeal in such cases will be sustained.

[1] Mayor v. Cooper, 6 Wall., 247; Hornthall v. The Collector, 9 Wall., 560; Blacklock v. Small, 127 U. S., 96; Citizens' Bank v. Carmon, 164 U. S., 319.

[2] Trustees v. Grenough, 105 U. S., 527.

[3] Freeman v. Alderson, 119 U. S., 185.

CLXXXVII. If a decree decides the merits of a controversy and also awards or refuses costs, and upon appeal the decree is reversed upon the merits, the appellate court will consider errors assigned upon the question of costs, but will not reverse the ruling of the trial court, unless a manifest abuse of discretion is shown.

Dobson v. Hartford Carpet Co., 114 U. S., 439; Dobson v. Dornan, 118 U. S., 10.

CLXXXVIII. As a suit in equity may involve separable controversies arising out of the matters presented by the complainant's bill, or upon a cross-bill filed by the defendant, or out of matters presented by intervening bills or petitions, it results that there may be several final and therefore appealable decrees rendered in the same case.

Each decree must be viewed with reference to the particular issue or controversy it deals with in determining its finality, and when a decree, final as to the issue or controversy it deals with, is rendered in a suit involving two or more controversies, the time allowed for taking an appeal therefrom dates from the entry of that particular decree; or, in other words, the time limit begins to run against each appealable decree from the date of its entry.

CLXXXIX. If the adversary parties in a cause each desire to take an appeal from an order or decree therein, separate appeals should be perfected on behalf of the complainant and defendant parties.

An appeal on behalf of one side to a controversy

takes up only errors against the appellant, and if the adversary party thereto does not also appeal, he is deemed to admit the correctness of the decree appealed from.[1]

A cross-appeal on behalf of an appellee may be allowed after the case has been carried up to the appellate court, but must be taken within the time allowed for taking an original appeal, and the same requirements with regard to assignment of errors, allowance, notice, and security must be observed as in case of an original appeal;[2] but a transcript of the record filed in the appellate court by one of the appealing parties may be used by the other, thus avoiding the cost of filing two transcripts of the same record.[3]

[1] Chittenden v. Brewster, 2 Wall., 191; S. S. Osborne, 105 U. S., 447; Mackal v. Mackal, 135 U. S., 167; Gage v. Pumpelly, 115 U. S., 454; Cherokee Nation v. Blackfeather, 155 U. S., 218.
[2] Farrar v. Churchill, 135 U. S., 609.
[3] Revised Statutes, section 1013.

CXC. If two or more decrees are entered in the same suit, affecting the same controversy, and doubt exists with respect to the finality of the earlier decree or decrees, it is advisable to take an appeal from each one, and usually successive appeals thus taken can be heard as one in the appellate court.

CXCI. As the transcript of the record must be filed in the appellate court not later than the return day named in the citation, the appellant, as soon as the appeal is allowed, should direct the clerk of the trial court to prepare the transcript and forward it to the clerk of the appellate court.

CXCII. To be effectual the appeal must be taken within the period fixed by statute for taking the same, and an appeal, for this purpose, is properly perfected by filing in the court from which the appeal is sought the necessary papers constituting an appeal, which ordinarily include the petition for and allowance of the appeal, the assignment of errors, the appeal bond approved, and the citation duly served.

<small>Credit Co. v. Arkansas Central Ry. Co., 128 U. S., 258.</small>

CXCIII. Strictly speaking, as an appeal is a right conferred by statute, the only step absolutely required to be taken, within the time limited for taking an appeal, in order to confer jurisdiction upon the appellate tribunal, is the obtaining an allowance of the appeal with notice thereof in some form to the adversary party.

<small>Dodge v. Knowles, 114 U. S., 430; Hewitt v. Filbert, 116 U. S., 142; Brown v. McConnell, 124 U. S., 489; Credit Co. v. Arkansas Central Ry. Co., 128 U. S., 258; Evans v. State Bank, 134 U. S., 330.</small>

CXCIV. The fact that an appeal has been allowed is proven if the record shows an appeal prayed for and allowed in open court during the term at which the order or decree sought to be appealed from was entered, or if it shows the filing of a petition for appeal and an allowance thereof by a judge or justice competent to grant the same.

It may be inferred from the fact that an appeal bond has been approved and a citation has been signed by a judge competent so to do,[1] or from the latter act only.[2]

[1] Sage v. Railroad Co., 96 U. S., 712; Draper v. Davis, 102 U. S., 370; Brandies v. Cochrane, 105 U. S., 262; Credit Co. v. Arkansas Central Ry. Co., 128 U. S., 258.

[2] Hewitt v. Filbert, 116 U. S., 142; Brown v. McConnell, 124 U. S., 489.

CXCV. Notice of the appeal to the adversary party is assumed, without service of a citation, if the appeal is allowed in open court at the term at which the order or decree sought to be appealed from was entered, provided the transcript of the record is duly filed within the required time in the appellate court.

CXCVI. If the appeal is allowed after the term, then notice thereof must be given by the issuance and service of a citation,[1] unless the appellee, in writing, acknowledges notice or waives service of citation or enters a general appearance in the case in the appellate court.[2]

[1] Dodge v. Knowles, 114 U. S., 430; Hewitt v. Filbert, 116 U. S., 142; Brown v. McConnell, 124 U. S., 489.

[2] Alviso v. United States, 5 Wall., 824; Sage v. Railroad Co., 96 U. S., 712; Richardson v. Green, 130 U. S., 104.

CXCVII. If steps sufficient to confer jurisdiction on appeal in the appellate tribunal have been taken, but the appeal has not been perfected through failure to give notice to the appellee, or to file the required security approved by the court, or to docket the case on appeal, or to pay the sum required to be paid to the clerk of the appellate court, an application must be made to that court for leave to perfect the appeal, and if the defect is in matter of mere procedure, the court may grant leave to perfect the same, and may also grant leave to amend the record in matters of form, or to correct mistakes in names, or to describe more fully the parties, or other like matters, when the amendment is in furtherance of justice and will not prejudice or injure the adversary party.

Revised Statutes, section 1005. Moore v. Simonds, 100 U. S., 145; United States v. Schoverling, 146 U. S., 76; Walton v. Marietta Chair Co., 157 U. S., 342.

CXCVIII. Although, from the authorities cited in connection with the past few paragraphs, it appears that jurisdiction on appeal may be conferred by acts falling short of a perfected appeal, relief being grantable to supply matters of mere procedure, the safer and better practice is to file in the trial court within the time allowed for taking the appeal a proper assignment of errors, and then cause the record to show the allowance of an appeal by either having the same allowed in open court during the term at which the order or decree appealed from is entered, or by filing a petition praying an appeal with the allowance thereof indorsed thereon by the proper judge, and in the latter case file the citation after due service upon the appellee, and also file a bond in the required amount, properly conditioned and approved by the judge.

CXCIX. If from any cause an appeal attempted to be taken is not perfected, so as to enable the appellate court to take jurisdiction, or the same is dismissed for a failure to observe the rules governing appeals, and the time allowed for taking an appeal has not expired, a second appeal may be taken, which will be entertained by the appellate court, if jurisdiction is obtained in the appellate court within the time allowed for an appeal.

Evans v. State Bank, 134 U. S., 330.

CHAPTER XX.

PROCEEDINGS IN APPELLATE COURTS — TRANSCRIPT — DOCKETING CASE.

CC. It is the duty of the appellant to docket the case and file the record thereof with the clerk of the appellate court by or before the return day, whether the same falls in vacation or in term time; but for good cause shown, the judge or justice who signed the citation, or any judge or justice of the appellate court, may enlarge the time for filing the record, by or before the expiration thereof, the order therefor to be filed with the clerk of the appellate court. Upon filing the record, the appellant must give security, or otherwise satisfy the clerk of the appellate court, for his fees.

Supreme Court Rule 9; Circuit Courts of Appeals Rule 16.

CCI. If the appellant fails to file the record and docket the case within the required time, the appellee may have the case docketed and dismissed upon producing a certificate, either in term time or vacation, from the clerk of the trial court, showing that an appeal in the case had been duly allowed; and if the appellee thus procures a dismissal of the case, the appellant cannot subsequently file the record and docket the case, unless leave so to do is obtained from the appellate court.

The appellee has the option, in case of a failure on part of the appellant, to docket the case and file a copy of the record, when the case stands for argument.

Supreme Court Rule 9; Circuit Courts of Appeals Rule 16.

CCII. The transcript or record, to be complete, must contain in itself, and not by reference, a perfect copy of the pleadings, and of all papers, exhibits, depositions or testimony however preserved, and any matters appearing of record necessary to bring the controversy fully before the appellate court, including the decrees or orders appealed from; and if any part of the proceedings are in a foreign language, the record must contain a translation thereof, made under the authority of the trial court or admitted by the adversary party to be correct, and the transcript must have annexed thereto a copy of the opinion or opinions filed in the trial court, and also the assignment of errors and the papers constituting the appeal, and must be duly certified to by the clerk, with the seal of the court attached.

Supreme Court Rules 8, 11; Circuit Courts Rules 14, 15; Railroad Co. v. Dinsmore, 108 U. S., 30.

CCIII. If the transcript filed in the appellate court is imperfect in that there has been omitted therefrom some material or necessary part of the record, as the same exists in the trial court, a motion, suggesting a diminution of the record, may be filed in the appellate court, asking the issuance of a *certiorari* to the trial court directing that the omitted portion of the record be forthwith certified up to the appellate court. The motion must be verified by affidavit, unless the facts upon which it is based are admitted by the other party, and must be made at the first term of the entry of the case in the appellate court, or otherwise the same will not be granted, unless the delay in applying for the same is accounted for to the satisfaction of the appellate court.

Supreme Court Rule 14; Circuit Courts of Appeal Rules 18.

CCIV. Upon docketing a case in an appellate court, the appellant must cause the record to be printed in the manner and within the time specified in the rules of the court; must prepare and print a proper brief and argument and file copies thereof with the clerk; must be in attendance upon the court when the case is reached upon call of the docket, if an oral argument is desired, and must, in all other respects, meet the requirements of the rules governing the court to which the appeal lies; and the appellee must in like manner prepare, print and file with the clerk a brief and argument, and be in attendance when the case is called, if he wishes to be heard orally. For the details governing the practice in the appellate court, reference must be had to the rules adopted by the particular court in which the case is pending. The rules of the supreme court, together with the rules in equity, are made part of this Manual, but the rules in force in the several circuits are not attached, as the same could not be included without greatly increasing the size of the Manual. The rules of the several circuit courts of appeal, fully annotated, will be found prefixed to volume 78 of the Federal Reporter.

CCV. After the final determination of the case in the appellate court, a mandate issues therefrom, the time of issuance being regulated by the rules of the particular court, to the circuit court from which the appeal was taken, for the purpose of informing that court of the decision reached by the appellate court, and, when necessary, for the purpose of directing the action of the trial court in the further progress of the case. It is the duty of the circuit court to record the mandate and to follow its directions.

Supreme Court Rules 39; Circuit Courts of Appeals Rules 32; Circuit Courts of Appeals Rules, 7th Circuit, 30. Kingsbury v. Buckner, 134 U. S., 650.

CHAPTER XXI.

THE ENFORCEMENT OF PROCESS AND DECREE—AUXILIARY PROCEEDINGS.

CCVI. When proper cause therefor exists, the court may enforce obedience to its process or orders by the issuance of writs of attachment for the arrest of the person of the disobedient party, or by the issuance of writs of sequestration for the seizure of his property.

Rule 8.

CCVII. Every person who, not being a party in a cause, has obtained an order, or in whose favor an order has been made, is entitled to enforce obedience to the same as if he were a party to the suit; and every person, not a party to the cause, against whom obedience to any order of the court may be enforced, shall be liable to the same process for enforcing obedience to such order that he would be were he a party to the cause.

Rule 10.

CCVIII. In those states wherein judgments in the courts of the state are liens upon the property of the debtor, the like effect is given to judgments rendered in the United States courts. Hence in such states a decree adjudging a sum certain to be due and ordering payment, being in effect a judgment, becomes a lien upon the property of the debtor.[1]

Prior to the adoption of the act of August 1, 1888,

it was held that the lien was co-extensive with the jurisdiction of the court rendering the judgment or decree.

By the provisions of that act it is declared that judgments or decrees rendered in the circuit or district courts of the United States shall be liens on property throughout the state in the same manner, to the same extent, and under the same conditions only, as if such judgments ordered had been rendered by a court of general jurisdiction of such state; provided, however, that whenever the laws of a state require a judgment or decree of a state court to be registered, docketed, indexed, or any other thing to be done in a particular manner, or in a certain office or county, or in the state of Louisiana in any parish, before the lien attaches, the provisions of the act should be applicable to the judgments and decrees of the United States courts in such state, only when the laws of the state authorizes the judgments and decrees of the United States courts to be registered, recorded, docketed, indexed or otherwise conformed to the requirements of the state law.[2]

[1] Massingill v. Downs, 7 How., 760; Ward v. Chamberlain, 2 Black, 430.
[2] 25 Statutes at Large, 357; 28 Statutes at Large, 814.

CCIX. Where, by the terms of the decree, specific property is ordered to be sold, as in mortgage foreclosures and like cases, it is customary to direct such sale to be made by a master named in the decree, which should also provide for the manner and terms of the sale, which are largely controlled by the provisions of the act of March 3, 1893, which require sales of realty to be at the court-house of the county, parish or city in which the property or greater part thereof is situated, or on the premises if the court so orders.

A certified copy of the decree should be furnished to the master named, as the evidence of his authority to proceed in the premises.

In conducting such sale the master must fully observe and carry out the provisions of the decree touching such sale, and, when made, must promptly make and return into court a report in writing of the proceedings had.

If the property sold was required to be appraised as a condition of sale, the report should show the proceedings had in this regard, also the notice of sale given, the time and place of sale, whether the property was sold in parcels or as a whole, and to whom and for what sum the sale was made.

Upon the filing of the report of sale, a motion for the confirmation thereof should be filed, upon which the court will make an order that exceptions to the sale must be filed within a given time.

Pewabic Mining Co. v. Mason, 145 U. S., 349.

If exceptions to such sale are filed and for cause sustained, or if the court of its own motion deems the sale to be faulty in form, or inequitable in substance, the same will be set aside and a resale be ordered.

If exceptions are not filed and cause to the contrary does not appear, the court, at any time after the expiration of the time for filing exceptions, may approve the report and confirm the sale, and order a conveyance of the property executed by the master to be delivered to the purchaser. If the sale is subject to redemption, the conveyance cannot be delivered until the expiration of the time of redemption. In such cases the master should execute a certificate of purchase and deliver the same to the purchaser. Upon the expiration of the period of redemption, if redemption has not been made, a brief report showing the fact, with the proper master's deed, should be submitted to the court for its approval, and for the order of delivery.

If redemption of the property has been made, then a report showing such fact should be returned by the master, upon which the proper orders and entries will be made by the court.

CCX. If by decree the payment of money be ordered, the same may be enforced by the issuance of a writ of execution in the form proper in an action at law in *assumpsit*.[1] If there are two or more districts in a state, the writ can be executed in either of the districts.

If the decree be for the performance of a specific act, as for the execution of a conveyance of land, the delivering up or cancellation of deeds or contracts, or other like act, the decree must prescribe the time within which the act must be done, and, in default thereof, upon affidavit of the complainant showing such default, the clerk issues a writ of attachment against the delinquent party, from which he cannot be released except upon full compliance with the decree and the payment of all costs, unless the court or judge, upon motion and affidavit, shall enlarge the time for performance.¹

If the delinquent party cannot be found, a writ of sequestration issues against his estate to compel obedience to the decree.¹

If the decree is for the delivery of possession of property, upon proof made by affidavit that the party refuses obedience to the decree upon demand made, a writ of assistance issues to enforce the delivery of possession, or otherwise to enforce the decree.²

This is the appropriate remedy to enforce the delivery of possession of property sold upon foreclosure of mortgage after the delivery of the master's deed.²

If a party is ousted from or deprived of the possession of property by force of a decree which is subsequently reversed, the court, upon entry of the order of reversal, will make all necessary orders for the restoration of the property, or its proceeds if sold, to the party wrongfully deprived thereof, and when necessary will issue a writ of restitution for that purpose, or upon summary hearing upon notice may enter judgment for money collected on the judgment subsequently reversed.[3]

[1] Rule 8.
[2] Rule 9. Terrell v. Allison, 21 Wall., 280; Root v. Woolworth, 150 U. S., 401.
[3] Northwestern Fuel Co. v. Brock, 139 U. S., 216.

CCXI. Upon the rendition of an interlocutory or final order or decree, if the defendant refuses or neglects to obey the same, and cannot be found within the jurisdiction of the court, so that obedience to the decree may be enforced by attachment of his person, a writ of sequestration may be issued against the estate of such delinquent defendant for the purpose of compelling obedience to the decree.

The proper practice is to file in the clerk's office the affidavit of complainant showing the non-compliance on part of defendant with the order or decree, and thereupon to procure the issuance by the clerk of a writ of attachment for the person of the defendant, which should be placed in the hands of the marshal for service. If service thereof cannot be had, by reason of not finding the defendant, the marshal must make return of such fact upon the writ of attachment, and thereupon complainant should file a petition in the cause reciting the rendition of the decree, the failure of defendant to obey the same, the issuance of the writ of attachment, and the return thereof unserved because the defendant cannot be found, and the fact that the defendant has property within the jurisdiction of the court, and submit the same to the court for its order thereon.

The writ is directed to the party or parties selected to act as sequestrators, directing and commanding them to take possession of the estate, or named portions thereof, of the delinquent defendant, and to hold the same, and the proceeds, rents and profits thereof, until the further order of court.

The rents and profits, and, if sold by order of court, the proceeds of the property, if sequestered, may be applied to the satisfaction of the decree, although primarily the object sought by the seizure of the property is the compelling the defendant to perform or yield obedience to the order or decree.

Rules 7, 8.

CCXII. Under the general rule that a court of equity has jurisdiction to enforce its decrees, coextensive with its jurisdiction to hear and decree the rights of the parties, it is held that the circuit court has full power, not only to issue all proper process, but to entertain all ancillary or auxiliary proceedings needed to fully enforce its decrees.

Jurisdiction over bills and proceedings of this character is not defeated by the citizenship of the parties thereto, as the jurisdiction is sustained by that of the original cause.

Minnesota Co. v. St. Paul Co., 2 Wall., 609; Terrell v. Allison, 21 Wall., 289; Krippendorf v. Hyde, 110 U. S., 276; Railroad Co. v. Railroad Co., 111 U. S., 505; Dewey v. Coal Co., 123 U. S., 329; Rouse v. Letcher, 156 U. S., 47; Gregory v. Van Ee, 160 U. S., 643; Carey v. Houston, etc., Ry. Co., 161 U. S., 115.

CCXIII. For the purpose of preserving in proper form the evidence of the proceedings had in suits in equity, upon the termination of a cause, a final record thereof containing the process, return of service, the pleadings, the decree and all other proceedings necessary to show the jurisdiction of the court, the regularity of the proceedings, and the results obtained, should be duly entered upon the records of the court.

Revised Statutes, section 750.

CCXIV. Under the provisions of section 918 of the Revised Statutes, the circuit courts have full power to make rules regulating the practice in suits in equity, not inconsistent with the laws of the United States or the rules prescribed by the supreme court.

Regard must therefore be had in each district to the special rules, if any, adopted by the circuit court for the district, touching the preparation and bringing to trial of suits in equity.

RULES OF PRACTICE

FOR THE

COURTS OF EQUITY

OF

THE UNITED STATES.

RULE I.

Court always open.— The circuit courts, as courts of equity, shall be deemed always open for the purpose of filing bills, answers and other pleadings; for issuing and returning mesne and final process and commissions; and for making and directing all interlocutory motions, orders, rules, and other proceedings, preparatory to hearing of all causes upon their merits.

RULE II.

Rule day.— The clerk's office shall be open, and the clerk shall be in attendance therein, on the first Monday of every month, for the purpose of receiving, entering, entertaining and disposing of all motions, rules, orders and other proceedings, which are grantable of course and applied for, or had by the parties or their solicitors, in all causes pending in equity, in pursuance of the rules hereby prescribed.

RULE III.

Orders at chambers.— Any judge of the circuit court, as well in vacation as in term, may at chambers, or on the rule days, at the clerk's office, make and direct all such interlocutory orders, rules and other proceedings, preparatory to the hearing of all causes upon their merits, in the same manner and with the same effect as the circuit court could make and direct the same in term, reasonable notice of the application therefor being first given to the adverse party or his solicitor to appear and show cause to the contrary at the next rule day thereafter, unless some other time is assigned by the judge for the hearing.

RULE IV.

Order book — Entry of motions.— All motions, rules, orders and other proceedings, made and directed at chambers, or on rule days at the clerk's office, whether special or of course, shall be entered by the clerk in an order book, to be kept at the clerk's office, on the day when they are made and directed; which book shall be open at all office hours to the free inspection of the parties in any suit in equity, and their solicitors. And except in cases where personal or other notice is specially required or directed, such entry in the order book shall be deemed sufficient notice to the parties and their solicitors, without further service thereof, of all orders, rules, acts, notices and other proceedings entered in such order book, touching any and all the matters in the suits to and in which they are parties and solicitors. And notice to the solicitors shall be deemed notice to the parties for whom they appear and whom they represent, in all cases where personal notice on the parties is not otherwise specially required. Where the solicitors for all the parties in a suit reside in or near the same town or city, the judges of the circuit court may, by rule, abridge the time for notice of rules, orders, or other proceedings not requiring personal service on the parties, in their discretion.

RULE V.

Motions grantable by clerk.— All motions and applications in the clerk's office for the issuing of mesne process and final process to enforce and execute decrees; for filing bills, answers, pleas, demurrers and other pleadings; for making amendments to bills and answers; for taking bills *pro confesso;* for filing exceptions; and for other proceedings in the clerk's office which do not, by the rules hereinafter prescribed, require any allowance or order of the court or of any judge thereof, shall be deemed motions and applications grantable of course by the clerk of the court. But the same may be suspended, or altered, or rescinded, by any judge of the court, upon special cause shown.

RULE VI.

Motions not of course.— All motions for rules or orders or other proceedings which are not grantable of course or without notice shall, unless a different time be assigned by a judge of the court, be made on a rule day, and entered in the order book, and shall be heard at the rule day next after that on which the motion is made. And if the adverse party, or his solicitor, shall not then appear, or shall not show good cause against the same, the motion may be heard by any judge of the court *ex parte*, and granted, as if not objected to, or refused, in his discretion.

RULE VII.

Mesne process.— The process of subpœna shall constitute the proper mesne process in all suits in equity, in the first instance, to require the defendant to appear and answer the exigency of the bill; and, unless otherwise provided in these rules, or specially ordered by the circuit court, a writ of attachment, and, if the defendant cannot be found, a writ of sequestration, or a writ of assistance to enforce a delivery of possession, as the case may require, shall be the proper process to issue for the purpose of compelling obedience to any interlocutory or final order or decree of the court.

RULE VIII.

Final process.—Final process to execute any decree may, if the decree be solely for the payment of money, be by a writ of execution in the form used in the circuit court in suits at common law in actions of *assumpsit*. If the decree be for the performance of any specific act, as, for example, for the execution of a conveyance of land or the delivering up of deeds or other documents, the decree shall, in all cases, prescribe the time within which the act shall be done, of which the defendant shall be bound, without further service, to take notice; and upon affidavit of the plaintiff, filed in the clerk's office, that the same has not been complied with within the prescribed time, the clerk shall issue a writ of attachment against the delinquent party, from which, if attached thereon, he shall not be discharged, unless upon a full compliance with the decree and the payment of all costs, or upon a special order of the court, or of a judge thereof, upon motion and affidavit, enlarging the time for the performance thereof. If the delinquent party cannot be found, a writ of sequestration shall issue against his estate upon the return of *non est inventus*, to compel obedience to the decree.

RULE IX.

Writ of assistance.—When any decree or order is for the delivery of possession, upon proof made by affidavit of a demand and refusal to obey the decree or order, the party prosecuting the same shall be entitled to a writ of assistance from the clerk of the court.

RULE X.

Persons not parties.—Every person, not being a party in any cause, who has obtained an order, or in whose favor an order shall have been made, shall be enabled to enforce obedience to such order by the same process as if he were a party to the cause; and every person, not being a party in any cause, against whom obedience to any order of the court may be enforced, shall be liable to the same process for enforcing obedience to such orders as if he were a party in the cause.

RULE XI.

Issuance of subpœna.— No process of subpœna shall issue from the clerk's office in any suit in equity until the bill is filed in the office.

RULE XII.

Return of subpœna.— Whenever a bill is filed, the clerk shall issue the process of subpœna thereon, as of course, upon the application of the plaintiff, which shall be returnable into the clerk's office the next rule day, or the next rule day but one, at the election of the plaintiff, occurring after twenty days from the time of the issuing thereof. At the bottom of the subpœna shall be placed a memorandum that the defendant is to enter his appearance in the suit in the clerk's office on or before the day at which the writ is returnable; otherwise the bill may be taken *pro confesso.* Where there are more than one defendant, a writ of subpœna may, at the election of the plaintiff, be sued out separately for each defendant, except in the case of husband and wife defendants, or a joint subpœna against all the defendants.

RULE XIII.

Manner of service of subpœna.— The service of all subpœnas shall be by a delivery of a copy thereof by the officer serving the same to the defendant personally, or by leaving a copy thereof at the dwelling-house or usual place of abode of each defendant, with some adult person who is a member or resident in the family.

RULE XIV.

Alias subpœna.— Whenever any subpœna shall be returned not executed as to any defendant, the plaintiff shall be entitled to another subpœna, *toties quoties,* against each defendant, if he shall require it, until due service is made.

RULE XV.

By whom served.— The service of all process, mesne and final, shall be by the marshal of the district, or his deputy, or by some other person specially appointed by the court for that purpose, and not otherwise. In the latter case, the person serving the process shall make affidavit thereof.

RULE XVI.

Docketing cause.— Upon the return of the subpœna as served and executed upon any defendant, the clerk shall enter the suit upon his docket as pending in the court, and shall state the time of the entry.

RULE XVII.

Appearance, when and how entered.— The appearance day of the defendant shall be the rule day to which the subpœna is made returnable, provided he has been served with the process twenty days before that day; otherwise his appearance day shall be the next rule day succeeding the rule day when the process is returnable.

The appearance of the defendant, either personally or by his solicitor, shall be entered in the order book on the day thereof by the clerk.

RULE XVIII.

Default and decree pro confesso.— It shall be the duty of the defendant, unless the time shall be otherwise enlarged, for cause shown, by a judge of the court, upon motion for that purpose, to file his plea, demurrer or answer to the bill in the clerk's office on the rule day next succeeding that of entering his appearance. In default thereof the plaintiff may, at his election, enter an order (as of course) in the order book that the bill be taken *pro confesso;* and thereupon the cause shall be proceeded in *ex parte,* and the matter of the bill may be decreed by the court at any time after the expiration of thirty days from and after the entry of said order if the same can be done without an answer, and is proper to be decreed; or the plaintiff, if he requires any discovery or answer to enable him to obtain a proper decree, shall be entitled to process of attachment against the defendant to compel an answer, and the defendant shall not, when arrested upon such process, be discharged therefrom, unless upon filing his answer, or otherwise complying with such order as the court or a judge thereof may direct, as to pleading to or fully answering the bill, within a period to be fixed by the court or judge, and undertaking to speed the cause.

RULE XIX.

Decree pro confesso — Default set aside.— When the bill is taken *pro confesso* the court may proceed to a decree at any time after the expiration of thirty days from and after the entry of the order to take the bill *pro confesso*, and such decree rendered shall be deemed absolute, unless the court shall, at the same term, set aside the same, or enlarge the time for filing the answer, upon cause shown, upon motion and affidavit of the defendant. And no such motion shall be granted unless upon the payment of the costs of the plaintiff in the suit up to that time, or such part thereof as the court shall deem reasonable, and unless the defendant shall undertake to file his answer within such time as the court shall direct, and submit to such other terms as the court shall direct, for the purpose of speeding the cause.

RULE XX.

Bill, form of.— Every bill, in the introductory part thereof, shall contain the names, places of abode and citizenship of all the parties, plaintiffs and defendants, by and against whom the bill is brought. The form, in substance, shall be as follows: " To the judges of the circuit court of the United States for the district of ——: A. B., of ——, and a citizen of the state of ——, brings this his bill against C. D., of ——, and a citizen of the state of ——, and E. F., of ——, and a citizen of the state of ——. And thereupon your orator complains and says that," etc.

RULE XXI.

Clauses omitted from bill.—The plaintiff, in his bill, shall be at liberty to omit, at his option, the part which is usually called the common confederacy clause of the bill, averring a confederacy between the defendants to injure or defraud the plaintiff; also what is commonly called the charging part of the bill, setting forth the matters or excuses which the defendant is supposed to intend to set up by way of defense to the bill; also what is commonly called the jurisdiction clause of the bill, that the acts complained of are contrary to equity, and that the defendant is without any remedy at law; and the bill shall not be demurrable therefor. And the plaintiff may, in the narrative or starting part of his bill, state and avoid, by counter-averments, at his option, any matter or thing which he supposes will be insisted upon by the defendant by way of defense or excuse to the case made by the plaintiff for relief. The prayer of the bill shall ask the special relief to which the plaintiff supposes himself entitled, and also shall contain a prayer for general relief; and if an injunction, or a writ of *ne exeat regno*, or any other special order, pending the suit, is required, it shall be specially asked for.

RULE XXII.

Parties beyond jurisdiction.—If any persons, other than those named as defendants in the bill, shall appear to be necessary or proper parties thereto, the bill shall aver the reason why they are not made parties, by showing them to be without the jurisdiction of the court, or that they cannot be joined without ousting the jurisdiction of the court as to the other parties. And as to persons who are without the jurisdiction and may properly be made parties, the bill may pray that process may issue to make them parties to the bill if they should come within the jurisdiction.

RULE XXIII.

Prayer for process.— The prayer for process of subpœna in the bill shall contain the names of the defendants named in the introductory part of the bill, and if any of them are known to be infants under age, or otherwise under guardianship, shall state the fact so that the court may take order thereon, as justice may require, upon the return of the process. If an injunction, or a writ of *ne exeat regno*, or any other special order, pending the suit, is asked for in the prayer for relief, that shall be sufficient, without repeating the same in the prayer for process.

RULE XXIV.

Counsel must sign bill.— Every bill shall contain the signature of counsel annexed to it, which shall be considered as an affirmation on his part that, upon the instructions given to him and the case laid before him, there is good ground for the suit in the manner in which it is framed.

RULE XXV.

Costs — Purposes of taxation.— In order to prevent unnecessary costs and expenses, and to promote brevity, succinctness and directness in the allegations of bills and answers, the regular taxable costs for every bill and answer shall in no case exceed the sum which is allowed in the state court of chancery in the district, if any there be; but if there be none, then it shall not exceed the sum of three dollars for every bill or answer.

RULE XXVI.

Contents of bill — Exceptions.— Every bill shall be expressed in as brief and succinct terms as it reasonably can be, and shall contain no unnecessary recitals of deeds, documents, contracts or other instruments, *in hæc verba*, or any other impertinent matter, or any scandalous matter not relevant to the suit. If it does, it may, on exceptions, be referred to a master by any judge of the court, for impertinence or scandal; and if so found by him, the matter shall be expunged at the expense of the plaintiff, and he shall pay to the defendant all his costs in the suit up to that time, unless the court or a judge thereof shall otherwise order. If the master shall report that the bill is not scandalous or impertinent, the plaintiff shall be entitled to all costs occasioned by the reference.

RULE XXVII.

Exceptions for scandal or impertinence.— No order shall be made by any judge for referring any bill, answer or pleading, or other matter or proceeding, depending before the court, for scandal or impertinence, unless exceptions are taken in writing and signed by counsel, describing the particular passages which are considered to be scandalous or impertinent; nor unless the exceptions shall be filed on or before the next rule day after the process on the bill shall be returnable, or after the answer or pleading is filed. And such order, when obtained, shall be considered as abandoned, unless the party obtaining the order shall, without any unnecessary delay, procure the master to examine and report on the same on or before the next succeeding rule day, or the master shall certify that further time is necessary for him to complete the examination.

RULE XXVIII.

Bills amended — Costs paid and copy furnished.— The plaintiff shall be at liberty, as a matter of course, and without payment of costs, to amend his bill, in any matters whatsoever, before any copy has been taken out of the clerk's office, and in any small matters afterwards, such as filling blanks, correcting errors of dates, misnomer of parties, misdescription of premises, clerical errors, and generally in matters of form. But if he amend in a material point, as he may do of course, after a copy has been so taken, before any answer or plea or demurrer to the bill, he shall pay to the defendant the costs occasioned thereby, and shall, without delay, furnish him a fair copy thereof, free of expense, with suitable references to the places where the same are to be inserted. And if the amendments are numerous, he shall furnish, in like manner, to the defendant, a copy of the whole bill as amended; and if there be more than one defendant, a copy shall be furnished to each defendant affected thereby.

RULE XXIX.

Amendment of bill.— After an answer or plea or demurrer is put in, and before replication, the plaintiff may, upon motion or petition, without notice, obtain an order from any judge of the court to amend his bill on or before the next succeeding rule day, upon payment of costs or without payment of costs, as the court or a judge thereof may in his discretion direct. But after replication filed, the plaintiff shall not be permitted to withdraw it and to amend his bill, except upon a special order of a judge of the court, upon motion or petition, after due notice to the other party, and upon proof by affidavit that the same is not made for the purpose of vexation or delay, or that the matter of the proposed amendment is material, and could not with reasonable diligence have been sooner introduced into the bill, and upon the plaintiff's submitting to such other terms as may be imposed by the judge for speeding the cause.

RULE XXX.

Abandonment and proceeding thereon.— If the plaintiff so obtaining any order to amend his bill after answer, or plea, or demurrer, or after replication, shall not file his amendments or amended bill, as the case may require, in the clerk's office on or before the next succeeding rule day, he shall be considered to have abandoned the same, and the cause shall proceed as if no application for any amendment had been made.

RULE XXXI.

Certificate of counsel — Affidavit.— No demurrer or plea shall be allowed to be filed to any bill unless upon a certificate of counsel that in his opinion it is well founded in point of law, and supported by the affidavit of the defendant that it is not interposed for delay; and if a plea, that it is true in point of fact.

RULE XXXII.

Defendant may demur, plead or answer.—The defendant may at any time before the bill is taken for confessed, or afterward with the leave of the court, demur or plead to the whole bill, or to part of it, and he may demur to part, plead to part and answer to the residue; but in every case in which the bill specially charges fraud or combination, a plea to such part must be accompanied with an answer fortifying the plea and explicitly denying the fraud and combination, and the facts on which the charge is founded.

RULE XXXIII.

Setting down for argument.—The plaintiff may set down the demurrer or plea to be argued, or he may take issue on the plea. If, upon an issue, the facts stated in the plea be determined for the defendant, they shall avail him as far as in law and equity they ought to avail him.

RULE XXXIV.

Proceedings on overruling demurrer or plea.—If, upon the hearing, any demurrer or plea is overruled, the plaintiff shall be entitled to his costs in the cause up to that period, unless the court shall be satisfied that the defendant has good ground, in point of law or fact, to interpose the same, and it was not interposed vexatiously or for delay. And, upon the overruling of any plea or demurrer, the defendant shall be assigned to answer the bill, or so much thereof as is covered by the plea or demurrer, the next succeeding rule day, or at such other period as, consistently with justice and the rights of the defendant, the same can, in the judgment of the court, be reasonably done; in default whereof, the bill shall be taken against him *pro confesso*, and the matter thereof proceeded in and decreed accordingly.

RULE XXXV.

If sustained — Amendment of bill.— If, upon the hearing, any demurrer or plea shall be allowed, the defendant shall be entitled to his costs. But the court may, in its discretion, upon motion of the plaintiff, allow him to amend his bill, upon such terms as it shall deem reasonable.

RULE XXXVI.

Extent of demurrer or plea.— No demurrer or plea shall be held bad and overruled upon argument, only because such demurrer or plea shall not cover so much of the bill as it might by law have extended to.

RULE XXXVII.

Answer as affecting demurrer or plea.— No demurrer or plea shall be held bad and overruled upon argument, only because the answer of the defendant may extend to some part of the same matter as may be covered by such demurrer or plea.

RULE XXXVIII.

Failure to reply or to set down for argument.— If the plaintiff shall not reply to any plea, or set down any plea or demurrer for argument, on the rule day when the same is filed, or on the next succeeding rule day, he shall be deemed to admit the truth and sufficiency thereof, and his bill shall be dismissed as of course unless a judge of the court shall allow him further time for the purpose.

RULE XXXIX.

Answer.— The rule that if a defendant submits to answer he shall answer fully to all the matters of the bill shall no longer apply in cases where he might by plea protect himself from such answer and discovery. And the defendant shall be entitled in all cases, by answer, to insist upon all matters of defense (not being matters of abatement, or to the character of the parties, or matters of form), in bar of or to the merits of the bill, of which he may be entitled to avail himself by a plea in bar; and in such answer he shall not be compellable to answer any other matters than he would be compellable to answer and discover upon filing a plea in bar and an answer in support of such plea, touching the matters set forth in the bill, to avoid or repel the bar or defense. Thus, for example, a *bona fide* purchaser for a valuable consideration, without notice, may set up that defense by way of answer instead of plea, and shall be entitled to the same protection and shall not be compellable to make any further answer or discovery of his title than he would be in any answer in support of such plea.

RULE XL.

Interrogatories.— It shall not hereafter be necessary to interrogate a defendant specially and particularly upon any statement in the bill, unless the complainant desires to do so to obtain a discovery.

RULE XLI.

Interrogatories continued.—(1) The interrogatories contained in the interrogating part of the bill shall be divided as conveniently as may be from each other, and numbered consecutively 1, 2, 3, etc.; and the interrogatories which each defendant is required to answer shall be specified in a note at the foot of the bill, in the form or to the effect following, that is to say: "The defendant (A. B.) is required to answer the interrogatories numbered respectively 1, 2, 3," etc.; and the office copy of the bill taken by each defendant shall not contain any interrogatories except those which such defendant is so required to answer, unless such defendant shall require to be furnished with a copy of the whole bill.

(2) If the complainant, in his bill, shall waive an answer under oath, or shall only require an answer under oath with regard to certain specified interrogatories, the answer of the defendant, though under oath, except such part thereof as shall be directly responsive to such interrogatories, shall not be

evidence in his favor, unless the cause be set down for hearing on bill and answer only; but may nevertheless be used as an affidavit, with the same effect as heretofore, on a motion to grant or dissolve an injunction, or on any other incidental motion in the cause; but this shall not prevent a defendant from becoming a witness in his own behalf under section 3 of the act of congress of July 2, 1864.

RULE XLII.

Note specifying interrogatories to be answered, part of bill.— The note at the foot of the bill, specifying the interrogatories which each defendant is required to answer, shall be considered and treated as part of the bill, and the addition of any such note to the bill, or any alteration in or addition to such note, after the bill is filed, shall be considered and treated as an amendment of the bill.

RULE XLIII.

Form when interrogatories are used.— Instead of the words of the bill now in use, preceding the interrogating part thereof, and beginning with the words: "To the end, therefore," there shall hereafter be used words in the form or to the effect following: "To the end, therefore, that the said defendants may, if they can, show why your orator should not have the relief hereby prayed, and may, upon their several and respective corporal oaths, and according to the best and utmost of their several and respective knowledge, remembrance, information and belief, full, true, direct and perfect answer make to such of the several interrogatories hereinafter numbered and set forth as by the note hereunder written they are respectively required to answer; that is to say —

"1. Whether, etc.
"2. Whether," etc.

RULE XLIV.

When interrogatories need not be answered.— A defendant shall be at liberty, by answer, to decline answering any interrogatory, or part of an interrogatory, from answering which he might have protected himself by demurrer; and he shall be at liberty so to decline, notwithstanding he shall answer other parts of the bill from which he might have protected himself by demurrer.

RULE XLV.

Special replication not allowed.—No special replication to any answer shall be filed. But if any matter alleged in the answer shall make it necessary for the plaintiff to amend his bill, he may have leave to amend the same with or without payment of costs, as the court, or a judge thereof, may in his discretion direct.

RULE XLVI.

Answer to amended bill.—In every case where an amendment shall be made after answer filed, the defendant shall put in a new or supplemental answer on or before the next succeeding rule day after that on which the amendment or bill is filed, unless the time is enlarged or otherwise ordered by a judge of the court; and upon his default, the like proceedings may be had as in cases of an omission to put in an answer.

RULE XLVII.

Omission of parties.—In all cases where it shall appear to the court that persons, who might otherwise be deemed necessary or proper parties to the suit, cannot be made parties by reason of their being out of the jurisdiction of the court, or incapable otherwise of being made parties, or because their joinder would oust the jurisdiction of the court as to the parties before the court, the court may in their discretion proceed in the cause without making such persons parties; and in such cases the decree shall be without prejudice to the rights of the absent parties.

RULE XLVIII.

Parties, when numerous.—Where the parties on either side are very numerous, and cannot, without manifest inconvenience and oppressive delays in the suit, be all brought before it, the court, in its discretion, may dispense with making all of them parties, and may proceed in the suit, having sufficient parties before it to represent all the adverse interests of the plaintiffs and the defendants in the suit properly before it. But, in such cases, the decree shall be without prejudice to the rights and claims of all the absent parties.

RULE XLIX.

Suits by trustees.— In all suits concerning real estate which is vested in trustees by devise, and such trustees are competent to sell and give discharges for the proceeds of the sale, and for the rents and profits of the estate, such trustees shall represent the persons beneficially interested in the estate, or the proceeds, or the rents and profits, in the same manner and to the same extent as the executors or administrators in suits concerning personal estate represent the persons beneficially interested in such personal estate; and in such cases it shall not be necessary to make the persons beneficially interested in such real estate, or rents and profits, parties to the suit; but the court may, upon consideration of the matter on the hearing, if it shall so think fit, order such persons to be made parties.

RULE L.

Heir, when party, and when not.— In suits to execute the trusts of a will, it shall not be necessary to make the heir at law a party; but the plaintiff shall be at liberty to make the heir at law a party where he desires to have the will established against him.

RULE LI.

Joint and several demands.— In all cases in which the plaintiff has a joint and several demand against several persons, either as principals or sureties, it shall not be necessary to bring before the court as parties to a suit concerning such demand all the persons liable thereto; but the plaintiff may proceed against one or more of the persons severally liable.

RULE LII.

Defect of parties.— Where the defendant shall, by his answer, suggest that the bill is defective for want of parties, the plaintiff shall be at liberty, within fourteen days after answer filed, to set down the cause for argument upon that objection only: and the purpose for which the same is so set down shall be notified by an entry, to be made in the clerk's order book, in the form or to the effect following (that is to say): "Set down upon the defendant's objection for want of parties." And where the plaintiff shall not so set down his cause, but shall proceed therewith to a hearing, notwithstanding an objection for want of parties taken by the answer, he shall not, at the hearing of the cause, if the defendant's objection shall then be allowed, be entitled as of course to an order for liberty to amend his bill by adding parties. But the court, if it thinks fit, shall be at liberty to dismiss the bill.

RULE LIII.

Objection of defect of parties.— If a defendant shall, at the hearing of a cause, object that a suit is defective for want of parties, not having by plea or answer taken the objection, and therein specified by name or description of parties to whom the objection applies, the court, if it shall think fit, shall be at liberty to make a decree saving the rights of the absent parties.

RULE LIV.

Nominal parties.— Where no account, payment, conveyance or other direct relief is sought against a party to a suit, not being an infant, the party, upon service of the subpœna upon him, need not appear and answer the bill, unless the plaintiff specially requires him so to do by the prayer of his bill; but he may appear and answer at his option; and if he does not appear and answer he shall be bound by all the proceedings in the cause. If the plaintiff shall require him to appear and answer he shall be entitled to the costs of all the proceedings against him, unless the court shall otherwise direct.

RULE LV.

Injunctions.— Whenever an injunction is asked for by the bill to stay proceedings at law, if the defendant do not enter his appearance, and plead, demur or answer to the same within the time prescribed therefor by these rules, the plaintiff shall be entitled, as of course, upon motion, without notice, to such injunction. But special injunctions shall be grantable only upon due notice to the other party by the court in term, or by a judge thereof in vacation, after a hearing, which may be *ex parte*, if the adverse party does not appear at the time and place ordered. In every case where an injunction — either the common injunction or a special injunction — is awarded in vacation, it shall, unless previously dissolved by the judge granting the same, continue until the next term of the court, or until it is dissolved by some other order of the court.

RULE LVI.

Revivor of suit.— Whenever a suit in equity shall become abated by the death of either party, or by any other event, the same may be revived by a bill of revivor, or a bill in the nature of a bill of revivor, as the circumstances of the case may require, filed by the proper parties entitled to revive the same, which bill may be filed in the clerk's office at any time, and, upon suggestion of the facts, the proper process of subpoena shall, as of course, be issued by the clerk requiring the proper representatives of the other party to appear and show cause, if any they have, why the cause should not be revived. And if no cause shall be shown at the next rule day which shall occur after fourteen days from the time of the service of the same process, the suit shall stand revived, as of course.

RULE LVII.

Supplemental bill.— Whenever a suit in equity shall become defective from any event happening after the filing of the bill, as, for example, by change of interest in the parties, or for any other reason, a supplemental bill, or a bill in the nature of a supplemental bill, may be necessary to be filed in the cause, leave to file the same may be granted by any judge of the court on any rule day, upon proper cause shown and due notice to the other party. And if leave is granted to file such supplemental bill, the defendant shall demur, plead or answer thereto on the next succeeding rule day after the supplemental bill is filed in the clerk's office, unless some other time shall be assigned by a judge of the court.

RULE LVIII.

Bills of revivor or supplement.— It shall not be necessary in any bill of revivor or supplemental bill to set forth any of the statements in the original suit, unless the special circumstances of the case may require it.

RULE LIX.

Answer verified before whom.— Every defendant may swear to his answer before any justice or judge of any court of the United States, or before any commissioner appointed by any circuit court to take testimony or depositions, or before any master in chancery appointed by any circuit court, or before any judge of any court of a state or territory, or notary public.

RULE LX.

Amendment of answer.— After an answer is put in it may be amended as of course in any matter of form or by filling up a blank, or correcting a date, or reference to a document, or other small matter, and be resworn, at any time before a replication is put in, or the cause is set down for a hearing upon bill and answer. But after replication or such setting down for a hearing it shall not be amended in any material matters, as by adding new facts or defenses, or qualifying or altering the original statements, except by special leave of the court, or of a judge thereof, upon motion and cause shown, after due notice to the adverse party, supported, if required, by affidavit; and in every case where leave is so granted, the court or the judge granting the same may, in his discretion, require that the same be separately engrossed, and added as a distinct amendment to the original answer, so as to be distinguishable therefrom.

RULE LXI.

Exceptions for insufficiency.— After an answer is filed on any rule day the plaintiff shall be allowed until the next succeeding rule day to file in the clerk's office exceptions thereto for insufficiency, and no longer, unless a longer time shall be allowed for the purpose, upon cause shown to the court, or a judge thereof; and, if no exception shall be filed thereto within that period, the answer shall be deemed and taken to be sufficient.

RULE LXII.

Costs of separate answers.— When the same solicitor is employed for two or more defendants, and separate answers shall be filed, or other proceedings had, by two or more of the defendants separately, costs shall not be allowed for such separate answers, or other proceedings, unless a master, upon reference to him, shall certify that such separate answers and other proceedings were necessary or proper, and ought not to have been joined together.

RULE LXIII.

Setting down exceptions for argument.— Where exceptions shall be filed to the answer for insufficiency, within the period prescribed by these rules, if the defendant shall not submit to the same and file an amended answer on the next succeeding rule day, the plaintiff shall forthwith set them down for a hearing on the next succeeding rule day thereafter, before a judge of the court, and shall enter, as of course, in the order book, an order for that purpose; and if he shall not so set down the same for a hearing, the exceptions shall be deemed abandoned, and the answer shall be deemed sufficient; provided, however, that the court, or any judge thereof, may, for good cause shown, enlarge the time for filing exceptions, or for answering the same, in his discretion, upon such terms as he may deem reasonable.

RULE LXIV.

If exceptions sustained, further answer.—If, at the hearing, the exceptions shall be allowed, the defendant shall be bound to put in a full and complete answer thereto on the next succeeding rule day; otherwise the plaintiff shall, as of course, be entitled to take the bill, so far as the matter of such exceptions is concerned, as confessed, or, at his election, he may have a writ of attachment to compel the defendant to make a better answer to the matter of the exceptions; and the defendant, when he is in custody upon such writ, shall not be discharged therefrom but by an order of the court, or of a judge thereof, upon his putting in such answer, and complying with such other terms as the court or judge may direct.

RULE LXV.

Costs on exceptions.—If, upon argument, the plaintiff's exceptions to the answer shall be overruled, or the answer shall be adjudged insufficient, the prevailing party shall be entitled to all the costs occasioned thereby, unless otherwise directed by the court, or the judge thereof, at the hearing upon the exceptions.

RULE LXVI.

Replication.—Whenever the answer of the defendant shall not be excepted to, or shall be adjudged or deemed sufficient, the plaintiff shall file the general replication thereto on or before the next succeeding rule day thereafter; and in all cases where the general replication is filed, the cause shall be deemed, to all intents and purposes, at issue, without any rejoinder or other pleading on either side. If the plaintiff shall omit or refuse to file such replication within the prescribed period, the defendant shall be entitled to an order, as of course, for a dismissal of the suit; and the suit shall thereupon stand dismissed, unless the court, or a judge thereof, shall, upon motion, for cause shown, allow a replication to be filed *nunc pro tunc*, the plaintiff submitting to speed the cause, and to such other terms as may be directed.

RULE LXVII.

Testimony—How taken.—(1) After the cause is at issue, commissions to take testimony may be taken out in vacation as well as in term, jointly by both parties, or severally by either party, upon interrogatories filed by the party taking out the same in the clerk's office, ten days' notice thereof being given to the adverse party to file cross-interrogatories before the issuing of the commission; and if no cross-interrogatories are filed at the expiration of the time, the commission may issue *ex parte*. In all cases the commissioner or commissioners shall be named by the court or by a judge thereof. Ordered, that the sixty-seventh rule governing equity practice be so amended as to allow the presiding judge of any court exercising jurisdiction, either in term time or in vacation, to vest in the clerk of said court general power to name commissioners to take testimony in like manner that the court or judge thereof can now do by the said sixty-seventh rule.

(2) Either party may give notice to the other that he desires the evidence to be adduced in the cause to be taken orally, and thereupon all the witnesses to be examined shall be examined before one of the examiners of the court or before an examiner to be specially appointed by the court, the examiner, if he so request, shall be furnished with a copy of the pleadings; and such examination shall take place in the presence of the parties or their agents, by their counsel or solicitors, and the witnesses shall be subject to cross-examination and re-examination, and which shall be conducted as near as may be in the mode now used in common-law courts. The depositions taken upon such oral examinations shall be reduced to writing by the examiner, in the form of question put and answer given; provided, that by consent of parties, the examiner may take down the testimony of any witness in the form of narrative.

At the request of either party, with reasonable notice, the deposition of any witness shall, under the direction of the examiner, be taken down either by a skilful stenographer or by a skilful typewriter, as the examiner may elect, and when taken stenographically shall be put into typewriting or other writing; provided, that such stenographer or typewriter has been appointed by the court, or is approved by both parties.

The testimony of each witness, after such reduction to writing, shall be read over to him and signed by him in the presence of the examiner and of such of the parties or counsel as may attend; provided, that if the witness shall refuse to sign his deposition so taken, then the examiner shall sign the same, stating upon the record the reasons, if any, assigned by the witness for such refusal.

The examiner may, upon all examinations, state any special matters to the court as he shall think fit; and any question or questions which may be objected to shall be noted by the examiner upon the deposition, but he shall not have power to decide on the competency, materiality or relevancy of the questions; and the court shall have power to deal with the costs of incompetent, immaterial or irrelevant depositions, or parts of them, as may be just.

In case of refusal of witnesses to attend, to be sworn, or to answer any question put by the examiner, or by counsel or solicitor, the same practice shall be adopted as is now practiced with respect to witnesses to be produced on examination before an examiner of said court on written interrogatories.

Notice shall be given by the respective counsel or solicitors to the opposite counsel or solicitors, or parties, of the time and place of the examination, for such reasonable time as the examiner may fix by order in each cause.

When the examination of witnesses before the examiner is concluded, the original depositions, authenticated by the signature of the examiner, shall be transmitted by him to the clerk of the court, to be there filed of record, in the same mode as prescribed in section 865 of the Revised Statutes.

Testimony may be taken on commission in the usual way,

by written interrogatories and cross-interrogatories, on motion to the court in term time, or to a judge in vacation, for special reasons, satisfactory to the court or judge.

Where the evidence to be adduced in a cause is to be taken orally, as before provided, the court may, on motion of either party, assign a time within which the complainant shall take his evidence in support of the bill, and a time thereafter within which the defendant shall take his evidence in defense, and a time thereafter within which the complainant shall take his evidence in reply; and no further evidence shall be taken in the cause, unless by agreement of the parties or by leave of court first obtained, on motion for cause shown.

The expense of the taking down of depositions by a stenographer and of putting them into typewriting or other writing shall be paid in the first instance by the party calling the witness, and shall be imposed by the court, as part of the costs, upon such party as the court shall adjudge should ultimately bear them.

Upon due notice given as prescribed by previous order, the court may, at its discretion, permit the whole, or any specific part, of the evidence to be adduced orally in open court on final hearing.

RULE LXVIII.

Under acts of congress.— Testimony may also be taken in the cause, after it is at issue, by deposition, according to the acts of congress. But in such case, if no notice is given to the adverse party of the time and place of taking the deposition, he shall, upon motion and affidavit of the fact, be entitled to a cross-examination of the witness, either under a commission or by a new deposition taken under the acts of congress, if a court or judge thereof shall, under all the circumstances, deem it reasonable.

RULE LXIX.

Time for testimony.— Three months, and no more, shall be allowed for the taking of testimony after the cause is at issue, unless the court, or a judge thereof, shall, upon special cause shown by either party, enlarge the time: and no testimony taken after such period shall be allowed to be read in evidence at the hearing. Immediately upon the return of the commissions and depositions containing the testimony into the clerk's office, publication thereof may be ordered in the clerk's office, by any judge of the court, upon due notice to the parties, or it may be enlarged, as he may deem reasonable under all the circumstances; but, by consent of the parties, publication of the testimony may at any time pass into the clerk's office, such consent being in writing, and a copy thereof entered in the order books, or indorsed upon the deposition or testimony.

RULE LXX.

Infirm, single or about to depart.—After any bill filed, and before the defendant hath answered the same, upon affidavit made that any of plaintiff's witnesses are aged and infirm, or going out of the country, or that any one of them is a single witness to a material fact, the clerk of the court shall, as of course, upon the application of the plaintiff, issue a commission to such commissioner or commissioners as a judge of the court may direct, to take the examination of such witness or witnesses *de bene esse*, upon giving due notice to the adverse party of the time and place of taking his testimony.

RULE LXXI.

Last interrogatory.—The last interrogatory in the written interrogatories to take testimony now commonly in use shall in the future be altered, and stated in substance thus: "Do you know, or can you set forth, any other matter or thing which may be a benefit or advantage to the parties at issue in this cause, or either of them, or that may be material to the subject of this your examination, or the matters in question in this cause? If yea, set forth the same fully and at large in your answer."

RULE LXXII.

Cross-bill — Answer to.— Where a defendant in equity files a cross-bill for discovery only against the plaintiff in the original bill, the defendant to the original bill shall first answer thereto before the original plaintiff shall be compellable to answer the cross-bill. The answer of the original plaintiff to such cross-bill may be read and used by the party filing the cross-bill at the hearing, in the same manner and under the same restrictions as the answer praying relief may now be read and used.

RULE LXXIII.

Account of estate.— Every decree for an account of the personal estate of a testator or intestate shall contain a direction to the master, to whom it is referred to take the same, to inquire and state to the court what parts, if any, of such personal estate are outstanding or undisposed of, unless the court shall otherwise direct.

RULE LXXIV.

Proceedings on reference.— Whenever any reference of any matter is made to a master to examine and report thereon, the party at whose instance or for whose benefit the reference was made shall cause the same to be presented to the master for hearing on or before the next rule day succeeding the time when the reference is made; if he shall omit to do so, the adverse party shall be at liberty forthwith to cause proceedings to be had before the master, at the costs of the party procuring the reference.

RULE LXXV.

Master, proceedings before.— Upon every such reference, it shall be the duty of the master, as soon as he reasonably can after the same is brought before him, to assign a time and place for proceedings in the same, and to give due notice thereof to each of the parties, or their solicitors; and if either party shall fail to appear at the time and place appointed the master shall be at liberty to proceed *ex parte*, or, in his discretion, to adjourn the examination and proceedings to a future day, giving notice to the absent party or his solicitor of such adjournment; and it shall be the duty of the master to proceed with all reasonable diligence in every such reference, and with the least practicable delay, and either party shall be at liberty to apply to the court, or a judge thereof, for an order to the master to speed the proceedings and to make his report, and to certify to the court or judge the reasons for any delay.

RULE LXXVI.

Master's report.— In the reports made by the master to the court, no part of any state of facts, charge, affidavit, deposition, examination or answer brought in or used before them shall be stated or recited. But such state of facts, charges, affidavits, deposition, examination or answer shall be identified, specified and referred to, so as to inform the court what state of facts, charge, affidavit, deposition or answer were so brought in or used.

RULE LXXVII.

Duty and power of master.— The master shall regulate all the proceedings in every hearing before him upon every such reference; and he shall have full authority to examine the parties in the cause, upon oath, touching all matters contained in the reference; and also to require the production of all books, papers, writings, vouchers and other documents applicable thereto; and also to examine on oath, *viva voce*, all witnesses produced by the parties before him, and to order the examination of other witnesses to be taken under a commission to be issued upon his certificate from the clerk's office or by deposition, according to the acts of congress, or otherwise, as hereinafter provided; and also to direct the mode in which the matters requiring evidence shall be proved before him; and generally to do all other acts, and direct all other inquiries and proceedings in the matters before him, which he may deem necessary and proper to the justice and merits thereof and the rights of the parties.

RULE LXXVIII.

Attendance of witnesses.— Witnesses who live within the district may, upon due notice to the opposite party, be summoned to appear before the commissioner appointed to take testimony, or before a master or examiner appointed in any cause, by subpœna in the usual form, which may be issued by the clerk in blank, and filled up by the party praying the same, or by the commissioner, master or examiner, requiring the attendance of the witnesses at the time and place specified, who shall be allowed for attendance the same compensation as for attendance in court; and if any witness shall refuse to appear or give evidence, it shall be deemed a contempt of the court, which being certified to the clerk's office by the commissioner, master or examiner, an attachment may issue thereupon by order of the court or of any judge thereof, in the same manner as if the contempt were for not attending, or for refusing to give testimony in the court. But nothing herein contained shall prevent the examination of witnesses *viva voce* when produced in open court, if the court shall, in its discretion, deem it advisable.

RULE LXXIX.

Form of accounts.— All parties accounting before a master shall bring in their respective accounts in the form of debtor and creditor; and any of the other parties who shall not be satisfied with the accounts so brought in shall be at liberty to examine the accounting party *viva voce*, or upon interrogatories, in the master's office, or by deposition, as the master shall direct.

RULE LXXX.

What used before master.— All affidavits, depositions and documents which have been previously made, read or used in the court, upon any proceeding in any cause or matter, may be used before the master.

RULE LXXXI.

Who may be examined.—The master shall be at liberty to examine any creditor or other person coming in to claim before him, either upon written interrogatories or *viva voce*, or in both modes, as the nature of the case may appear to require. The evidence upon such examinations shall be taken down by the master, or by some other person by his order and in his presence, if either party requires it, in order that the same may be used by the court, if necessary.

RULE LXXXII.

Appointment—Fees.—The circuit courts may appoint standing masters in chancery in their respective districts, both the judges concurring in the appointment; and they may also appoint a master *pro hac vice* in any particular case. The compensation to be allowed to every master in chancery for his services in any particular case shall be fixed by the circuit court, in its discretion, having regard to all the circumstances thereof, and the compensation shall be charged upon and borne by such of the parties in the cause as the court shall direct. The master shall not retain his report as security for his compensation; but, when the compensation is allowed by the court, he shall be entitled to an attachment for the amount against the party who is ordered to pay the same, if, upon notice thereof, he does not pay it within the time prescribed by the court.

RULE LXXXIII.

Return and entry of master's report.—The master, as soon as his report is ready, shall return the same into the clerk's office, and the day of the return shall be entered by the clerk in the order book. The parties shall have one month from the time of filing the report to file exceptions thereto, and, if no exceptions are within that period filed by either party, the report shall stand confirmed on the next rule day after the month is expired. If exceptions are filed they shall stand for hearing before the court if the court is then in session, or, if not, then at the next sitting of the court which shall be held thereafter, by adjournment or otherwise.

RULE LXXXIV.

Costs on frivolous causes.— And, in order to prevent exceptions to reports from being filed for frivolous causes, or for mere delay, the party whose exceptions are overruled shall, for every exception overruled, pay costs to the other party, and for every exception allowed shall be entitled to costs; the costs to be fixed in each case by the court, by a standing rule of the circuit court.

RULE LXXXV.

Correction of decree.— Clerical mistakes in decrees or decretal orders, or errors arising from any accidental slip or omission, may, at any time before an actual enrollment thereof, be corrected by order of the court or a judge thereof, upon petition, without the form or expense of a rehearing.

RULE LXXXVI.

Decree, form of.— In drawing up decrees and orders, neither the bill, nor answer, nor other pleadings, nor any part thereof, nor the report of any master, nor any other prior proceeding, shall be recited or stated in the decree or order; but the decree and order shall begin, in substance, as follows: "This cause came on to be heard (or to be further heard, as the case may be) at this term, and was argued by counsel; and thereupon, upon consideration thereof, it was ordered, adjudged and decreed as follows, viz.:" [Here insert the decree or order.]

RULE LXXXVII.

Suits by or against incompetents.— Guardians *ad litem* to defend a suit may be appointed by the court, or by any judge thereof, for infants or other persons who are under guardianship, or otherwise incapable to sue for themselves. All infants and other persons so incapable may sue by their guardians, if any, or by their *prochein ami;* subject, however, to such orders as the court may direct for them.

RULE LXXXVIII.

Rehearing.— Every petition for a rehearing shall contain the special matter or cause on which such rehearing is applied for, shall be signed by counsel, and the facts therein stated, if not apparent on the record, shall be verified by the oath of the party or by some other person. No rehearing shall be granted after the term at which the final decree of the court shall have been entered and recorded, if an appeal lies to the supreme court. But if no appeal lies, the petition may be admitted at any time before the end of the next term of the court in the discretion of the court.

RULE LXXXIX.

Rules by circuit court.— The circuit courts (a majority of all the judges thereof, including the justice of the supreme court, the circuit judges and the district judge for the district, concurring therein) may make any other and further rules and regulations for the practice, proceedings, and process, mesne and final, in their respective districts, not inconsistent with the rules hereby prescribed, in their discretion, and from time to time alter and amend the same.

RULE XC.

Rules of practice.— In all cases where the rules prescribed by this court or by the circuit court do not apply, the practice of the circuit court shall be regulated by the present practice of the high court of chancery in England, so far as the same may reasonably be applied consistently with the local circumstances and local conveniences of the district where the court is held, not as positive rules, but as furnishing just analogies to regulate the practice.

RULE XCI.

Affirmation.— Whenever, under these rules, an oath is or may be required to be taken, the party may, if conscientiously scrupulous of taking an oath, in lieu thereof make solemn affirmation to the truth of the facts stated by him.

RULE XCII.

Decree in foreclosure cases.— In suits in equity for the foreclosure of mortgages in the circuit court of the United States, or in any court of the Territories having jurisdiction of the same, a decree may be rendered for any balance that may be found due to the complainant over and above the proceeds of the sale or sales, and execution may issue for the collection of the same, as is provided in the eighth rule of this court regulating the equity practice, where the decree is solely for the payment of money.

RULE XCIII.

Injunction — On appeal.— When an appeal from a final decree, in an equity suit, granting or dissolving an injunction, is allowed by a justice or judge who took part in the decision of the cause, he may, in his discretion, at the time of such allowance, make an order suspending or modifying the injunction during the pendency of the appeal, upon such terms as to bond or otherwise as he may consider proper for the security of the rights of the opposite party.

RULE XCIV.

Bill by stockholder.— Every bill brought by one or more stockholders in a corporation, against the corporation and other parties, founded on rights which may properly be asserted by the corporation, must be verified by oath, and must contain an allegation that the plaintiff was a shareholder at the time of the transaction of which he complains, or that his share had devolved on him since, by operation of law, and that the suit is not a collusive one to confer on a court of the United States jurisdiction of a case of which it would not otherwise have cognizance. It must also set forth with particularity the efforts of the plaintiff to secure such action as he desires on the part of the managing directors or trustees, and, if necessary, of the shareholders, and the causes of his failure to obtain such action.

RULES

OF THE

SUPREME COURT OF THE UNITED STATES.

1.

CLERK.

1. The clerk of this court shall reside and keep the office at the seat of the national government, and he shall not practice, either as attorney or counselor, in this court or in any other court, while he shall continue to be clerk of this court.

2. The clerk shall not permit any original record or paper to be taken from the court room or from the office without an order from the court except as provided by rule 10.

2.

ATTORNEYS AND COUNSELORS.

1. It shall be requisite to the admission of attorneys or counselors to practice in this court that they shall have been such for three years past in the supreme courts of the states to which they respectively belong, and that their private and professional character shall appear to be fair.

2. They shall respectively take and subscribe the following oath or affirmation, viz.:

I, —— ——, do solemnly swear [or, affirm] that I will demean myself, as an attorney and counselor of this court, uprightly and according to law, and that I will support the constitution of the United States.

3.

PRACTICE.

This court considers the former practice of the courts of king's bench and of chancery, in England, as affording outlines for the practice of this court; and will, from time to time, make such alterations therein as circumstances may render necessary.

4.

BILL OF EXCEPTIONS.

The judges of the circuit and district courts shall not allow any bill of exceptions which shall contain the charge of the court at large to the jury in trials at common law, upon any general exception to the whole of such charge. But the party excepting shall be required to state distinctly the several matters of law in such charge to which he excepts; and those matters of law, and those only, shall be inserted in the bill of exceptions and allowed by the court.

5.

PROCESS.

1. All process of this court shall be in the name of the President of the United States.

2. When process at common law or in equity shall issue against a state, the same shall be served on the governor, or chief executive magistrate and attorney-general of such state.

3. Process of subpœna, issuing out of this court, in any suit in equity, shall be served on the defendant sixty days before the return-day of the said process; and if the defendant, on such service of the subpœna, shall not appear at the return-day, the complainant shall be at liberty to proceed *ex parte*.

6.

MOTIONS.

1. All motions to the court shall be reduced to writing, and shall contain a brief statement of the facts and objects of the motion.

2. One hour on each side shall be allowed to the argument of a motion, and no more, without special leave of the court, granted before the argument begins.

3. No motion to dismiss, except on special assignment by the court, shall be heard, unless previous notice has been given to the adverse party, or the counsel or attorney of such party.

4. All motions to dismiss writs of error and appeals, except motions to docket and dismiss under rule 9, must be submitted in the first instance on printed briefs or arguments. If the court desires further argument on that subject, it will be ordered in connection with the hearing on the merits. The party moving to dismiss shall serve notice of the motion, with a copy of his brief of argument, on the counsel for plaintiff in error or appellant of record in this court, at least three weeks before the time fixed for submitting the motion, in all cases except where the counsel to be notified resides west of the Rocky Mountains, in which case the notice shall be at least thirty days. Affidavits of the deposit in the mail of the notice and brief to the proper address of the counsel to be served, duly post-paid, at such time as to reach him by due course of mail the three weeks or thirty days before the time fixed by the notice, will be regarded as *prima facie* evidence of service on counsel who reside without the District of Columbia. On proof of such service, the motion will be considered, unless, for satisfactory reasons, further time be given by the court to either party.

5. There may be united, with a motion to dismiss a writ of error or an appeal, a motion to affirm on the ground that, although the record may show that this court has jurisdiction, it is manifest the writ or appeal was taken for delay only, or that the question on which the jurisdiction depends is so frivolous as not to need further argument.

6. The court will not hear arguments on Saturday (unless for special cause it shall order to the contrary), but will devote that day to the other business of the court. The motion-day shall be Monday of each week; and motions not required by the rules of the court to be put on the docket shall be entitled

to preference immediately after the reading of opinions, if such motions shall be made before the court shall have entered upon the hearing of a case upon the docket.

7.

LAW LIBRARY.

1. During the session of the court, any gentleman of the bar having a case on the docket, and wishing to use any book or books in the law library, shall be at liberty, upon application to the clerk of the court, to receive an order to take the same (not exceeding at any one time three) from the library, he being thereby responsible for the due return of the same within a reasonable time, or when required by the clerk. It shall be the duty of the clerk to keep, in a book for that purpose, a record of all books so delivered, which are to be charged against the party receiving the same. And in case the same shall not be so returned, the party receiving the same shall be responsible for and forfeit and pay twice the value thereof, and also one dollar per day for each day's detention beyond the limited time.

2. The clerk shall deposit in the law library, to be there carefully preserved, one copy of the printed record in every case submitted to the court for its consideration, and of all printed motions, briefs or arguments filed therein.

3. The marshal shall take charge of the books of the court, together with such of the duplicate law-books as congress may direct to be transferred to the court, and arrange them in the conference-room, which he shall have fitted up in a proper manner; and he shall not permit such books to be taken therefrom by any one except the justices of the court.

8.

WRIT OF ERROR, RETURN AND RECORD.

1. The clerk of the court to which any writ of error may be directed shall make return of the same, by transmitting a true copy of the record, and of the assignment of errors, and of all proceedings in the case, under his hand and the seal of the court.

2. In all cases brought to this court, by writ of error or appeal, to review any judgment or decree, the clerk of the court by which such judgment or decree was rendered shall annex to and transmit with the record a copy of the opinion or opinions filed in the case, and in cases at law a complete copy of the charge of the court to the jury.

3. No case will be heard until a complete record, containing in itself, and not by reference, all the papers, exhibits, depositions, and other proceedings which are necessary to the hearing in this court, shall be filed.

4. Whenever it shall be necessary or proper, in the opinion of the presiding judge in any circuit court, or district court exercising circuit-court jurisdiction, that original papers of any kind should be inspected in this court upon writ of error or appeal, such presiding judge may make such rule or order for the safe-keeping, transporting, and return of such original papers as to him may seem proper, and this court will receive and consider such original papers in connection with the transcript of the proceedings.

5. All appeals, writs of error, and citations must be made returnable not exceeding thirty days from the day of signing the citation, whether the return day fall in vacation or in term time, and be served before the return day.

6. The record in cases of admiralty and maritime jurisdiction, when under the requirements of law the facts have been found in the court below, and the power of review is limited to the determination of questions of law arising on the record, shall be confined to the pleadings, the findings of fact, and conclusions of law thereon, the bills of exceptions, the final judgment or decree, and such interlocutory orders and decrees as may be necessary to a proper review of the case.

9.

DOCKETING CASES.

1. It shall be the duty of the plaintiff in error or appellant to docket the case and file the record thereof with the clerk of this court by or before the return day, whether in vacation or

in term time. But, for good cause shown, the justice or judge who signed the citation, or any justice of this court, may enlarge the time, by or before its expiration, the order of enlargement to be filed with the clerk of this court. If the plaintiff in error or appellant shall fail to comply with this rule, the defendant in error or appellee may have the cause docketed and dismissed upon producing a certificate, whether in term time or vacation, from the clerk of the court wherein the judgment or decree was rendered, stating the case and certifying that such writ of error or appeal has been duly sued out or allowed. And in no case shall the plaintiff in error or appellant be entitled to docket the case and file the record after the same shall have been docketed and dismissed under this rule, unless by order of the court.

2. But the defendant in error or appellee may, at his option, docket the case and file a copy of the record with the clerk of this court; and, if the case is docketed and a copy of the record filed with the clerk of this court by the plaintiff in error or appellant within the period of time above limited and prescribed by this rule, or by the defendant in error or appellee at any time thereafter, the case shall stand for argument.

3. Upon the filing of the transcript of a record brought up by writ of error or appeal, the appearance of the counsel for the party docketing the case shall be entered.

4. In all cases where the period of thirty days is mentioned in rule 8, it shall be extended to sixty days in writs of error and appeals from California, Oregon, Nevada, Washington, New Mexico, Utah, Arizona, Montana, Wyoming, North Dakota, South Dakota, Alaska and Idaho.

10.

PRINTING RECORDS.

1. In all cases the plaintiff in error or appellant, on docketing a case and filing the record, shall enter into an undertaking to the clerk, with surety to his satisfaction, for the payment of his fees, or otherwise satisfy him in that behalf.

2. The clerk shall cause an estimate to be made of the cost of printing the record, and of his fee for preparing it for the printer and supervising the printing, and shall notify to the party docketing the case the amount of the estimate. If he shall not pay it within a reasonable time, the clerk shall notify the adverse party, and he may pay it. If neither party shall pay it, and for want of such payment the record shall not have been printed when a case is reached in the regular call of the docket, after March 1, 1884, the case shall be dismissed.

3. Upon payment by either party of the amount estimated by the clerk, twenty-five copies of the record shall be printed, under his supervision, for the use of the court and of counsel.

4. In cases of appellate jurisdiction the original transcript on file shall be taken by the clerk to the printer. But the clerk shall cause copies to be made for the printer of such original papers, sent up under rule 8, section 4, as are necessary to be printed; and of the whole record in cases of original jurisdiction.

5. The clerk shall supervise the printing, and see that the printed copy is properly indexed. He shall distribute the printed copies to the justices and the reporter, from time to time, as required, and a copy to the counsel for the respective parties.

6. If the actual cost of printing the record, together with the fee of the clerk, shall be less than the amount estimated and paid, the amount of the difference shall be refunded by the clerk to the party paying it. If the actual cost and clerk's fee shall exceed the estimate, the amount of the excess shall be paid to the clerk before the delivery of a printed copy to either party or his counsel.

7. In case of reversal, affirmance, or dismissal, with costs, the amount of the cost of printing the record and of the clerk's fee shall be taxed against the party against whom costs are given, and shall be inserted in the body of the mandate or other proper process.

8. Upon the clerk's producing satisfactory evidence, by affidavit or the acknowledgment of the parties or their sureties,

of having served a copy of the bill of fees due by them, respectively, in this court, on such parties or their sureties, an attachment shall issue against such parties or sureties, respectively, to compel payment of said fees.

9. The plaintiff in error or appellant may, within ninety days after filing the record in this court, file with the clerk a statement of the errors on which he intends to rely, and of the parts of the record which he thinks necessary for the consideration thereof, and forthwith serve on the adverse party a copy of such statement. The adverse party, within ninety days thereafter, may designate in writing, filed with the clerk, additional parts of the record which he thinks material; and, if he shall not do so, he shall be held to have consented to a hearing on the parts designated by the plaintiff in error or appellant. If parts of the record shall be so designated by one or both of the parties, the clerk shall print those parts only; and the court will consider nothing but those parts of the record, and the errors so stated. If at the hearing it shall appear that any material part of the record has not been printed, the writ of error or appeal may be dismissed, or such other order made as the circumstances may appear to the court to require. If the defendant in error or appellee shall have caused unnecessary parts of the record to be printed, such order as to costs may be made as the court shall think proper.

The fees of the clerk under rule 24, section 7, shall be computed, as at present, on the folios in the record as filed, and shall be in full for the performance of his duties in the execution hereof.

11.

TRANSLATIONS.

Whenever any record transmitted to this court upon a writ of error or appeal shall contain any document, paper, testimony, or other proceedings in a foreign language, and the record does not also contain a translation of such document, paper, testimony, or other proceeding, made under the authority of the inferior court, or admitted to be correct, the record shall not be printed; but the case shall be reported to this court by the clerk, and the court will thereupon remand it to the inferior court, in order that a translation may be there supplied and inserted in the record.

12.

FURTHER PROOF.

1. In all cases where further proof is ordered by the court, the depositions which may be taken shall be by a commission, to be issued from this court, or from any circuit court of the United States.

2. In all cases of admiralty and maritime jurisdiction, where new evidence shall be admissible in this court, the evidence by testimony of witnesses shall be taken under a commission to be issued from this court, or from any circuit court of the United States, under the direction of any judge thereof; and no such commission shall issue but upon interrogatories, to be filed by the party applying for the commission, and notice to the opposite party or his agent or attorney, accompanied with a copy of the interrogatories so filed, to file cross-interrogatories within twenty days from the service of such notice: Provided, however, that nothing in this rule shall prevent any party from giving oral testimony in open court in cases where by law it is admissible.

13.

OBJECTIONS TO EVIDENCE IN THE RECORD.

In all cases of equity or admiralty jurisdiction, heard in this court, no objection shall hereafter be allowed to be taken to the admissibility of any deposition, deed, grant, or other exhibit found in the record as evidence, unless objection was taken thereto in the court below and entered of record; but the same shall otherwise be deemed to have been admitted by consent.

14.

CERTIORARI.

No *certiorari* for diminution of the record will be hereafter awarded in any case, unless a motion therefor shall be made in writing, and the facts on which the same is founded shall, if not admitted by the other party, be verified by affidavit. And all motions for *certiorari* must be made at the first term of the entry of the case; otherwise, the same will not be granted, unless upon special cause shown to the court, accounting satisfactorily for the delay.

15.

DEATH OF A PARTY.

1. Whenever, pending a writ of error or appeal in this court, either party shall die, the proper representatives in the personalty or realty of the deceased party, according to the nature of the case, may voluntarily come in and be admitted parties to the suit, and thereupon the case shall be heard and determined as in other cases; and if such representatives shall not voluntarily become parties, then the other party may suggest the death on the record, and thereupon, on motion, obtain an order that unless such representatives shall become parties within the first ten days of the ensuing term, the party moving for such order, if defendant in error, shall be entitled to have the writ of error or appeal dismissed; and if the party so moving shall be plaintiff in error, he shall be entitled to open the record, and on hearing have the judgment or decree reversed, if it be erroneous: Provided, however, that a copy of every such order shall be printed in some newspaper of general circulation within the state, territory, or district from which the case is brought, for three successive weeks, at least sixty days before the beginning of the term of the supreme court then next ensuing.

2. When the death of a party is suggested, and the representatives of the deceased do not appear by the tenth day of the second term next succeeding the suggestion, and no meas-

ures are taken by the opposite party within that time to compel their appearance, the case shall abate.

3. When either party to a suit in a circuit court of the United States shall desire to prosecute a writ of error or appeal to the supreme court of the United States from any final judgment or decree rendered in the circuit court, and at the time of suing out such writ of error or appeal the other party to the suit shall be dead and have no proper representative within the jurisdiction of the court which rendered such final judgment or decree, so that the suit cannot be revived in that court, but shall have a proper representative in some state or territory of the United States, the party desiring such writ of error or appeal may procure the same, and may have proceedings on such judgment or decree superseded or stayed in the same manner as is now allowed by law in other cases, and shall thereupon proceed with such writ of error or appeal as in other cases. And within thirty days after the commencement of the term to which such writ of error or appeal is returnable, the plaintiff in error or appellant shall make a suggestion to the court, supported by affidavit, that the said party was dead when the writ of error or appeal was taken or sued out, and had no proper representative within the jurisdiction of the court which rendered said judgment or decree, so that the suit could not be revived in that court, and that said party had a proper representative in some state or territory of the United States, and stating therein the name and character of such representative, and the state or territory in which such representative resides; and, upon such suggestion, he may, on motion, obtain an order that, unless such representative shall make himself a party within the first ten days of the ensuing term of the court, the plaintiff in error or appellant shall be entitled to open the record, and, on hearing, have the judgment or decree reversed if the same be erroneous: Provided, however, that a proper citation reciting the substance of such order shall be served upon such representative, either personally or by being left at his residence, at least sixty days before the beginning of the term of

the supreme court then next ensuing: And provided, also, that in every such case, if the representative of the deceased party does not appear by the tenth day of the term next succeeding said suggestion, and the measures above provided to compel the appearance of such representative have not been taken within time as above required by the opposite party, the case shall abate: And provided, also, that the said representative may at any time before or after said suggestion come in and be made a party to the suit, and thereupon the case shall proceed, and be heard and determined as in other cases.

16.

NO APPEARANCE OF PLAINTIFF.

Where no counsel appears and no brief has been filed for the plaintiff in error or appellant, when the case is called for trial, the defendant may have the plaintiff called and the writ of error or appeal dismissed, or may open the record and pray for an affirmance.

17.

NO APPEARANCE OF DEFENDANT.

Where the defendant fails to appear when the case is called for trial, the court may proceed to hear an argument on the part of the plaintiff and to give judgment according to the right of the case.

18.

NO APPEARANCE OF EITHER PARTY.

When a case is reached in the regular call of the docket, and there is no appearance for either party, the case shall be dismissed at the cost of the plaintiff.

19.

NEITHER PARTY READY AT SECOND TERM.

When a case is called for argument at two successive terms, and upon the call at the second term neither party is prepared to argue it, it shall be dismissed at the cost of the plaintiff, unless sufficient cause is shown for further postponement.

20.

PRINTED ARGUMENTS.

1. In all cases brought here on writ of error, appeal, or otherwise, the court will receive printed arguments without regard to the number of the case on the docket, if the counsel on both sides shall choose to submit the same within the first ninety days of the term; and, in addition, appeals from the court of claims may be submitted by both parties within thirty days after they are docketed, but not after the 1st day of April; but twenty-five copies of the arguments, signed by attorneys or counselors of this court, must be first filed.

2. When a case is reached in the regular call of the docket, and a printed argument shall be filed for one or both parties, the case shall stand on the same footing as if there were an appearance by counsel.

3. When a case is taken up for trial upon the regular call of the docket, and argued orally in behalf of only one of the parties, no printed argument for the opposite party will be received, unless it is filed before the oral argument begins, and the court will proceed to consider and decide the case upon the *ex parte* argument.

4. No brief or argument will be received, either through the clerk or otherwise, after a case has been argued or submitted, except upon leave granted in open court after notice to opposing counsel.

21.

BRIEFS.

1. The counsel for plaintiff in error or appellant shall file with the clerk of the court, at least six days before the case is called for argument, twenty-five copies of a printed brief, one of which shall, on application, be furnished to each of the counsel engaged upon the opposite side.

2. This brief shall contain, in the order here stated —

(1) A concise abstract, or statement of the case, presenting succinctly the questions involved and the manner in which they are raised.

(2) A specification of the errors relied upon, which, in cases brought up by writ of error, shall set out separately and particularly each error asserted and intended to be urged; and in cases brought up by appeal the specification shall state, as particularly as may be, in what the decree is alleged to be erroneous. When the error alleged is to the admission or to the rejection of evidence, the specification shall quote the full substance of the evidence admitted or rejected. When the error alleged is to the charge of the court, the specification shall set out the part referred to *totidem verbis*, whether it be instructions given or instructions refused. When the error alleged is to a ruling upon the report of a master, the specification shall state the exception to the report and the action of the court upon it.

(3) A brief of the argument, exhibiting a clear statement of the points of law or fact to be discussed, with a reference to the pages of the record and the authorities relied upon in support of each point. When a statute of a state is cited, so much thereof as may be deemed necessary to the decision of the case shall be printed at length.

3. The counsel for a defendant in error or an appellee shall file with the clerk twenty-five printed copies of his argument, at least three days before the case is called for hearing. His brief shall be of like character with that required of the plaintiff in error or appellant, except that no specification of errors shall be required, and no statement of the case, unless that presented by the plaintiff in error or appellant is controverted.

4. When there is no assignment of errors, as required by section 997 of the Revised Statutes, counsel will not be heard, except at the request of the court; and errors not specified according to this rule will be disregarded; but the court, at its option, may notice a plain error not assigned or specified.

5. When, according to this rule, a plaintiff in error or an appellant is in default, the case may be dismissed on motion; and when a defendant in error or an appellee is in default, he will not be heard, except on consent of his adversary, and by request of the court.

6. When no oral argument is made for one of the parties, only one counsel will be heard for the adverse party.

22.

ORAL ARGUMENTS.

1. The plaintiff or appellant in this court shall be entitled to open and conclude the argument of the case. But when there are cross-appeals they shall be argued together as one case, and the plaintiff in the court below shall be entitled to open and conclude the argument.

2. Only two counsel will be heard for each party on the argument of a case.

3. Two hours on each side will be allowed for the argument, and no more, without special leave of the court, granted before the argument begins. The time thus allowed may be apportioned between the counsel on the same side, at their discretion: Provided, always, that a fair opening of the case shall be made by the party having the opening and closing arguments.

23.

INTEREST.

1. In cases where a writ of error is prosecuted to this court, and the judgment of the inferior court is affirmed, the interest shall be calculated and levied, from the date of the judgment below until the same is paid, at the same rate that similar judgments bear interest in the courts of the state where such judgment is rendered.

2. In all cases where a writ of error shall delay the proceedings on the judgment of the inferior court, and shall appear to have been sued out merely for delay, damages at a rate not exceeding ten per cent., in addition to interest, shall be awarded upon the amount of the judgment.

3. The same rule shall be applied to decrees for the payment of money in cases in equity, unless otherwise ordered by this court.

4. In cases in admiralty, damages and interest may be allowed if specially directed by the court.

24.

COSTS.

1. In all cases where any suit shall be dismissed in this court, except where the dismissal shall be for want of jurisdiction, costs shall be allowed to the defendant in error or appellee, unless otherwise agreed by the parties.

2. In all cases of affirmance of any judgment or decree in this court, costs shall be allowed to the defendant in error or appellee, unless otherwise ordered by the court.

3. In cases of reversal of any judgment or decree in this court, costs shall be allowed to the plaintiff in error or appellant, unless otherwise ordered by the court. The cost of the transcript of the record from the court below shall be a part of such costs, and be taxable in that court as costs in the case.

4. Neither of the foregoing sections shall apply to cases where the United States are a party; but in such cases no costs shall be allowed in this court for or against the United States.

5. In all cases of the dismissal of any suit in this court, it shall be the duty of the clerk to issue a mandate, or other proper process in the nature of a *procedendo*, to the court below, for the purpose of informing such court of the proceedings in this court, so that further proceedings may be had in such court as to law and justice may appertain.

6. When costs are allowed in this court, it shall be the duty of the clerk to insert the amount thereof in the body of the mandate, or other proper process sent to the court below, and annex to the same the bill of items taxed in detail.

7. In pursuance of the act of March 3, 1883, authorizing and empowering this court to prepare a table of fees to be charged by the clerk of this court, the following table is adopted:

For docketing a case and filing and indorsing the transcript of the record, five dollars.

For entering an appearance, twenty-five cents.

For entering a continuance, twenty-five cents.

For filing a motion, order, or other paper, twenty-five cents.

For entering any rule, or for making or copying any record or other paper, twenty cents per folio of each one hundred words.

For transferring each case to a subsequent docket and indexing the same, one dollar.

For entering a judgment or decree, one dollar.

For every search of the records of the court, one dollar.

For a certificate and seal, two dollars.

For receiving, keeping and paying money in pursuance of any statute or order of court, two per cent. on the amount so received, kept and paid.

For an admission to the bar and certificate under seal, ten dollars.

For preparing the record or a transcript thereof for the printer, indexing the same, supervising the printing and distributing the printed copies to the justices, the reporter, the law library, and the parties or their counsel, fifteen cents per folio.

For making a manuscript copy of the record, when required under rule 10, twenty cents per folio, but nothing in addition for supervising the printing.

For issuing a writ of error and accompanying papers, five dollars.

For a mandate or other process, five dollars.

For filing briefs, five dollars for each party appearing.

For every copy of any opinion of the court or any justice thereof, certified under seal, one dollar for every printed page, but not to exceed five dollars in the whole for any copy.

25.

OPINIONS OF THE COURT.

1. All opinions delivered by the court shall, immediately upon the delivery thereof, be handed to the clerk to be recorded. And it shall be the duty of the clerk to cause the same to be forthwith recorded, and to deliver a copy to the reporter as soon as the same shall be recorded.

2. The original opinions of the court shall be filed with the clerk of this court for preservation.

3. Opinions printed under the supervision of the justices delivering the same need not be copied by the clerk into a book of records; but at the end of each term the clerk shall cause such printed opinions to be bound in a substantial manner into one or more volumes, and when so bound they shall be deemed to have been recorded within the meaning of this rule.

26.

CALL AND ORDER OF THE DOCKET.

1. The court, on the second day in each term, will commence calling the cases for argument in the order in which they stand on the docket, and proceed from day to day during the term in the same order (except as hereinafter provided); and if the parties, or either of them, shall be ready when the case is called, the same will be heard: and if neither party shall be ready to proceed in the argument, the case shall go down to the foot of the docket, unless some good and satisfactory reason to the contrary shall be shown to the court.

2. Ten cases only shall be considered as liable to be called on each day during the term. But on the coming in of the court on each day the entire number of such ten cases will be called, with a view to the disposition of such of them as are not to be argued.

3. Criminal cases may be advanced by leave of the court on motion of either party.

4. Cases once adjudicated by this court upon the merits, and again brought up by writ of error or appeal, may be advanced by leave of the court on motion of either party.

5. Revenue and other cases in which the United States are concerned, which also involve or affect some matter of general public interest, may also by leave of the court be advanced on motion of the attorney-general.

6. All motions to advance cases must be printed, and must contain a brief statement of the matter involved, with the reasons for the application.

7. No other case will be taken up out of the order on the docket, or be set down for any particular day, except under special and peculiar circumstances to be shown to the court. Every case which shall have been called in its order and passed and put at the foot of the docket shall, if not again reached during the term it was called, be continued to the next term of the court.

8. Two or more cases, involving the same question, may, by the leave of the court, be heard together, but they must be argued as one case.

9. If, after a case has been passed under circumstances which do not place it at the foot of the docket, the parties shall desire to have it heard, they may file with the clerk their joint request to that effect, and the case shall then be by him reinstated for call ten cases after that under argument, or next to be called at the end of the day the request is filed. If the parties will not unite in such a request, either may move to take up the case, and it shall then be assigned to such place upon the docket as the court may direct.

10. No stipulation to pass a case without placing it at the foot of the docket will be recognized as binding upon the court. A case can only be so passed upon application made and leave granted in open court.

27.

ADJOURNMENT.

The court will, at every term, announce on what day it will adjourn at least ten days before the time which shall be fixed upon, and the court will take up no case for argument, nor receive any case upon printed briefs, within three days next before the day fixed upon for adjournment.

28.

DISMISSING CASES IN VACATION.

Whenever the plaintiff and defendant in a writ of error pending in this court, or the appellant and appellee in an appeal, shall in vacation, by their attorneys of record, sign and file with the clerk an agreement in writing directing the case to be dismissed, and specifying the terms on which it is to be dismissed, as to costs, and shall pay to the clerk any fees that may be due to him, it shall be the duty of the clerk to enter the case dismissed, and to give to either party requesting it a copy of the agreement filed; but no mandate or other process shall issue without an order of the court.

29.

SUPERSEDEAS.

Supersedeas bonds in the circuit courts must be taken, with good and sufficient security, that the plaintiff in error or appellant shall prosecute his writ or appeal to effect, and answer all damages and costs if he fail to make his plea good. Such indemnity, where the judgment or decree is for the recovery of money not otherwise secured, must be for the whole amount of the judgment or decree, including just damages for delay, and costs and interest on the appeal; but in all suits where the property in controversy necessarily follows the event of the suit, as in real actions, replevin, and in suits on mortgages, or where the property is in the custody of the marshal under admiralty process, as in case of capture or seizure, or where the proceeds thereof, or a bond for the value thereof, is in the custody or control of the court, indemnity in all such cases is only required in an amount sufficient to secure the sum recovered for the use and detention of the property, and the costs of the suit, and just damages for delay, and costs and interest on the appeal.

30.

REHEARING.

A petition for rehearing after judgment can be presented only at the term at which judgment is entered, unless by special leave granted during the term; and must be printed and briefly and distinctly state its grounds, and be supported by certificate of counsel; and will not be granted, or permitted to be argued, unless a justice who concurred in the judgment desires it, and a majority of the court so determines.

31.

FORM OF PRINTED RECORDS AND BRIEFS.

All records, arguments, and briefs printed for the use of the court must be in such form and size that they can be conveniently bound together, so as to make an ordinary octavo volume.

32.

WRITS OF ERROR AND APPEALS UNDER THE ACT OF FEBRUARY 25, 1889, CHAPTER 236, OR UNDER SECTION 5 OF THE ACT OF MARCH 3, 1891, CHAPTER 517.

Cases brought to this court by writ of error or appeal, under the act of February 25, 1889, chapter 236, or under section 5 of the act of March 3, 1891, chapter 517, where the only question in issue is the question of the jurisdiction of the court below, will be advanced on motion, and heard under the rules prescribed by rule 6, in regard to motions to dismiss writs of error and appeals.

33.

MODELS, DIAGRAMS, AND EXHIBITS OF MATERIALS.

1. Models, diagrams, and exhibits of material forming part of the evidence taken in the court below, in any case pending in this court, on writ of error or appeal, shall be placed in the custody of the marshal of this court at least one month before the case is heard or submitted.

2. All models, diagrams, and exhibits of material, placed in the custody of the marshal for the inspection of the court on the hearing of a case, must be taken away by the parties within one month after the case is decided. When this is not done, it shall be the duty of the marshal to notify the counsel in the case, by mail or otherwise, of the requirements of this

rule; and if the articles are not removed within a reasonable time after the notice is given, he shall destroy them, or make such other disposition of them as to him may seem best.

34.

CUSTODY OF PRISONERS ON HABEAS CORPUS.

1. Pending an appeal from the final decision of any court or judge declining to grant the writ of *habeas corpus*, the custody of the prisoner shall not be disturbed.

2. Pending an appeal from the final decision of any court or judge discharging the writ after it has been issued, the prisoner shall be remanded to the custody from which he was taken by the writ, or shall, for good cause shown, be detained in custody of the court or judge, or be enlarged upon recognizance as hereinafter provided.

3. Pending an appeal from the final decision of any court or judge discharging the prisoner, he shall be enlarged upon recognizance, with surety, for appearance to answer the judgment of the appellate court, except where, for special reasons, sureties ought not to be required.

35.

ASSIGNMENT OF ERRORS.

1. Where an appeal or a writ of error is taken from a district court or a circuit court direct to this court, under section 5 of the act entitled "An act to establish circuit courts of appeals and to define and regulate in certain cases the jurisdiction of the courts of the United States, and for other purposes," approved March 3, 1891, the plaintiff in error or appellant shall file with the clerk of the court below, with his petition for the writ of error or appeal, an assignment of errors, which shall set out separately and particularly each error asserted and intended to be urged. No writ of error or appeal shall be allowed until such assignment of errors shall have been filed. When the error alleged is to the admission

or to the rejection of evidence, the assignment of errors shall quote the full substance of the evidence admitted or rejected. When the error alleged is to the charge of the court, the assignment of errors shall set out the part referred to *totidem verbis*, whether it be in instructions given or in instructions refused. Such assignment of errors shall form part of the transcript of the record, and be printed with it. When this is not done counsel will not be heard, except at the request of the court; and errors not assigned according to this rule will be disregarded, but the court, at its option, may notice a plain error not assigned.

2. The plaintiff in error or appellant shall cause the record to be printed, according to the provisions of sections 2, 3, 4, 5, 6 and 9 of rule 10.

36.

APPEALS AND WRITS OF ERROR.

1. An appeal or a writ of error from a circuit court or a district court direct to this court, in the cases provided for in sections 5 and 6 of the act entitled "An act to establish circuit courts of appeals, and to define and regulate in certain cases the jurisdiction of the courts of the United States, and for other purposes," approved March 3, 1891, may be allowed, in term time or in vacation, by any justice of this court, or by any circuit judge within his circuit, or by any district judge within his district, and the proper security be taken and the citation signed by him, and he may also grant a *supersedeas* and stay of execution or of proceedings, pending such writ of error or appeal.

2. Where such writ of error is allowed in the case of a conviction of an infamous crime, or in any other criminal case in which it will lie under said sections 5 and 6, the circuit court or district court, or any justice or judge thereof, shall have power, after the citation is served, to admit the accused to bail in such amount as may be fixed.

37.

CASES FROM CIRCUIT COURT OF APPEALS.

1. Where, under section 6 of the said act, a circuit court of appeals shall certify to this court a question or proposition of law, concerning which it desires the instruction of this court for its proper decision, the certificate shall contain a proper statement of the facts on which such question or proposition of law arises.

2. If application is thereupon made to this court that the whole record and cause may be sent up to it for its consideration, the party making such application shall, as a part thereof, furnish this court with a certified copy of the whole of said record.

3. Where application is made to this court under section 6 of the said act to require a case to be certified to it for its review and determination, a certified copy of the entire record of the case in the circuit court of appeals shall be furnished to this court by the applicant, as part of the application.

38.

INTEREST, COSTS, AND FEES.

The provisions of rules 23 and 24 of this court, in regard to interest and costs and fees, shall apply to writs of error and appeals and reviews under the provisions of sections 5 and 6 of the said act.

39.

MANDATES.

Mandates shall issue as of course after the expiration of thirty days from the day the judgment or decree is entered, unless the time is enlarged by order of the court, or of a justice thereof when the court is not in session, but during the term.

FORMS.

BILL OF COMPLAINT.

In the United States Circuit Court in and for the —— District of ——. —— Term, 18—.

A. B.
   v.   } Equity.
C. D. and E. F.

To the Judges of the Circuit Court of the United States for the —— District of ——:

A. B., a citizen of the state of ——, residing in —— county in said state, brings this his bill against C. D., a citizen of the state of ——, residing in —— county in said state, and E. F., a citizen of the state of ——, residing in —— county in said state, and thereupon your orator complains and says that, etc.

[*Here insert cause of action.*]

To the end that your orator may obtain the relief to which he is justly entitled in the premises, he now prays the court to grant him due process by subpœna directed to said C. D. and E. F., defendants hereinbefore named, requiring and commanding each of them to appear herein and answer under oath [*or, but not under oath, the same being expressly waived*] the several allegations in this your orator's bill contained.

And your orator further prays that upon the final hearing it be ordered and decreed that [*here insert the special relief sought*].

And further prays for such other and further relief as may be just and equitable.   A. B.,
   X. Y.,   By X., Y. and Z.,
      Of Counsel.   His Solicitors.

If a writ of *ne exeat* is desired the reasons for asking therefor should be set out immediately following the prayer for the process by subpœna, with the prayer —

Wherefore your orator prays the court to grant him a writ of *ne exeat* restraining and forbidding said C. D., defendant herein, from departing beyond the limits of the United States without leave of this court first had.

If an injunction is desired pending the trial, a prayer for the issuance thereof should be added immediately following the prayer for process.

If the grounds therefor have not already been fully set forth in the bill, the same should be set forth followed by the prayer —

Wherefore your orator prays the court to now grant him a writ of injunction restraining and enjoining the said defendants from [*here insert the special matters desired to be enjoined*], until the further order and decree of this court in the premises.

PRÆCIPE FOR PROCESS.

[*Entitle as before.*]
To Clerk of said Court:

In above cause, being a bill filed for [*here state briefly purpose of bill, as for foreclosure of mortgage, or to set aside conveyance of realty*], please issue a subpœna to C. D. and E. F., defendants, returnable on the rule day in [*here insert the name of month*]. X. Y.,
Solicitor for Complainant.

If for any reason it is desired to issue separate subpœnas the *præcipe* should so direct.

ENTRY OF APPEARANCE IN PERSON.

[*Entitle as before.*]
To Clerk of said Court:

Please enter my appearance as defendant in above cause on the —— rule day [*or as of the date of the filing hereof*].

ENTRY OF APPEARANCE BY SOLICITOR.

[*Entitle as before.*]
To Clerk of said Court:

In above cause please enter the appearance of —— ——, defendant, and of myself as his solicitor, on the —— rule day [*or as of the date of the filing hereof*].

GENERAL DEMURRER.

[*Entitle case as before.*]
The demurrer of C. D. and E. F., defendants.

These defendants, not confessing all or any of the matters in the bill of complaint contained to be true as therein set forth, do demur to said bill for that the same does not state such a case, nor contain any matter of equity, entitling the complainant to any relief against these defendants. Wherefore they pray the judgment of the court whether they shall be compelled to further answer said bill, and further pray to be dismissed with their costs.

—— ——.
—— ——.

I, —— ——, of counsel for the defendants in the above cause, do hereby certify that the foregoing demurrer to the bill of complaint is in my opinion well founded in law.

UNITED STATES OF AMERICA, }
    District of ——. }

I, —— ——, defendant in the above cause, being duly sworn, do say that the foregoing demurrer to the bill of complaint is not interposed for purposes of delay.

Subscribed and sworn to before me this —— day of ——.

—— ——.

SPECIAL DEMURRER TO BILL.

[*Entitle case as before.*]
The demurrer of C. D. and E. F., defendants.

These defendants, not confessing all or any of the matters and things in the bill of complaint contained to be true as therein alleged, do demur to said bill, and for cause thereof showeth that, etc. [*here set forth specifically the grounds of demurrer*].

Wherefore they pray the judgment of the court whether they shall be compelled to further answer said bill. And further pray to be dismissed. with costs.

[*Add certificate and affidavit as before.*]

DEMURRER TO PART OF BILL.

[*Entitle case as before.*]

The demurrer of C. D. and E. F. to part of bill.

These defendants, not confessing all or any of the matters and things in the bill of complaint contained to be true as therein alleged, do demur to so much of said bill as [*here describe the part or parts of bill demurred to, and set forth the grounds of demurrer thereto*].

Wherefore defendants pray the judgment of the court whether they shall be compelled to further answer make to said parts of the bill herein demurred to.

[*Add certificate and affidavit as before.*]

PLEA TO BILL.

[*Entitle as before.*]

The plea of C. D. and E. F. to the bill of complaint.

These defendants, not confessing all or any of the matters in said bill of complaint to be true as therein alleged, for plea to said bill aver and say [*here set forth the matter of the plea*].

All of which matters and things these defendants do aver to be true, and plead the same in bar [*or, in abatement, as the case may be*] of complainant's said bill, and pray the judgment of the court whether they shall be compelled to further answer said bill, and pray to be hence dismissed with costs.

I, —— ——, of counsel for defendants in above cause, do certify that the foregoing plea to the bill of complaint is in my opinion well founded in law.

UNITED STATES OF AMERICA, }
    District of ——.

I, —— ——, defendant in the above cause, being duly sworn, do say that the foregoing plea to the bill of complaint is true in point of fact, and is not interposed for purposes of delay.

Subscribed and sworn to before me this —— day of ——.

—— ——.

PLEA TO PART OF BILL.

[*Entitle as before.*]

The plea of C. D. and E. F., defendants, to part of said bill.

These defendants, not confessing all or any of the matters in said bill of complaint contained to be true as therein alleged, for plea to so much and such part of said bill as [*here describe part pleaded to*], aver and say that [*here set forth the matter of the plea*], all of which matters and things these defendants do aver to be true, and they plead the same to so much of said bill as is hereinbefore described, and pray the judgment of the court whether they shall be required to further answer so much of said bill as is covered by this plea.

[*Add certificate and affidavit as before.*]

DEMURRER, PLEA AND ANSWER IN ONE.

[*Entitle as before.*]

Demurrer, plea and answer of E. F. and C. D., defendants.

I. These defendants, not confessing all or any of the matters and things in said bill contained to be true as therein alleged, do demur to so much of said bill of complaint as [*here describe parts of bill to which the demurrer applies*], and for cause of demurrer do show that [*here set forth grounds of demurrer*].

Wherefore they pray judgment of this court whether they shall be required to further answer the parts of said bill demurred to.

II. And the said defendants, not waiving the foregoing demurrer, but wholly relying thereon, as to so much of said bill as [*here insert description of parts of bill to which plea is interposed*], do plead thereto, and for cause thereof do aver and say that [*here set forth the grounds of plea*]. All of which matters the said defendants do plead to so much of said bill as is herein last above mentioned, and pray the judgment of this court whether they shall be compelled to further answer said parts of said bill thus pleaded to.

III. And the said defendants, not waiving their said demurrer and plea, but relying thereon, for answer to so much of said bill as they are advised it is material and necessary to answer unto, do say that [*here set forth the matters necessary to be stated in response to the bill, as well as matters of defense*].

Wherefore these defendants pray to be hence dismissed with costs.

[*Add certificate and affidavit as to demurrer and plea.*]

ANSWER TO BILL.

[*Entitle as before.*]

The answer of C. D. and E. F., defendants to the bill of complaint.

These defendants, saving and reserving unto themselves the benefit of all exceptions to the errors and imperfections in said bill contained, for answer to so much thereof as they are advised it is necessary or material for them to answer unto, do aver and say that [*here insert the matters responsive to the bill, as well as the matters of defense*].

And having thus fully made answer to said bill, these defendants pray to be hence dismissed with costs.

UNITED STATES OF AMERICA, }
    District of ———.

We, ——— ——— and ——— ———, defendants in above cause, having read the foregoing answer, and being each duly sworn, do say that the matters and things in said answer contained are true.

Subscribed and sworn to before me this ——— day of ———.

——— ———.

EXCEPTIONS FOR SCANDAL OR IMPERTINENCE.

[*Entitle as before.*]

Exceptions taken to the bill [*or answer*] in said cause filed for expunging the scandalous [*or impertinent*] matter therein contained.

Complainant [*or defendant*] excepts to so much of said bill [*or answer*] as is included within [*here describe the passages or parts excepted to*], for that the same is scandalous [*or impertinent*], for which reason the complainant [*or defendant*] excepts to said bill [*or answer*], and prays that such scandalous [*or impertinent*] matter be expunged therefrom.

X. Y.,
Solicitor for ——.

EXCEPTIONS TO ANSWER FOR INSUFFICIENCY.

[*Entitle as before.*]

Exceptions for insufficiency to the answer of C. D. and E. F., defendants in above cause.

Complainant excepts to the answer of said defendants herein filed [*or to so much of said answer, describing same*] for insufficiency, for that [*here insert the grounds of exception*]. For which reasons the said answer is insufficient and incomplete and ought to be amended, and complainant prays that the same be amended accordingly.

REPLICATION TO ANSWER.

[*Entitle as before.*]

Replication of complainant in above cause to the answer of C. D. and E. F., defendants.

This repliant, saving and reserving all advantage of exception to the manifold insufficiencies of said answer, for replication thereto saith that he will aver and prove his said bill to be true and sufficient, and that the said answer is untrue and insufficient; wherefore he prays relief as in said bill set forth.

PRÆCIPE FOR SUBPŒNA TO WITNESS.

[*Entitle as before.*]
To Clerk of said Court:

In above entitled cause in equity please issue subpœna to F. G., a witness on behalf of ——, directing him to appear and testify before —— ——, commissioner, at ——, on the ——.

X. Y.,
Solicitor for ——.

PRÆCIPE FOR COMMISSION ON INTERROGATORIES.

[*Entitle as before.*]
To Clerk of said Court:

In above entitled cause in equity please select some proper person as commissioner and issue a *dedimus* to him authorizing him to take the testimony of F. G. and H. K., upon the interrogatories filed in your office for that purpose. Witnesses reside at ——.

X. Y.,
Solicitor for ——.

PRÆCIPE FOR SETTING DOWN CAUSE FOR ARGUMENT OR HEARING.

[*Entitle as before.*]
To Clerk of said Court:

In above cause set down for argument demurrer [*or*, plea] filed to the bill.

Set down above cause for argument on defendant's objection for want of parties.

Set down above cause for hearing on bill and answer.

Set down above cause for hearing on pleadings and proofs.

PETITION FOR APPEAL.

[*Entitle as before.*]

Your petitioner, the —— in the above entitled cause, would respectfully represent and show that in the above entitled case pending in the United States circuit court in and for the —— district of ——, there was entered at the —— term, 18—, of said court, a final decree greatly to the prejudice and injury of your petitioner, which said decree is erroneous and inequitable in many particulars.

Wherefore, in order that your petitioner may obtain relief in the premises and have opportunity to show the errors complained, your petitioner prays that he may be allowed an appeal in said case to the —— court, and that the proper orders touching the security required of him may be made.

CITATION.

United States of America, To —— ——:

You are hereby notified that in a certain case in equity in the United States circuit court in and for the —— district of ——, wherein —— —— is complainant and —— —— and —— —— are defendants, an appeal has been allowed the —— therein to the ——, and you are hereby cited and admonished to be and appear in said court at ——, —— days after the date of this citation, to show cause, if any there be, why the order and decree appealed from should not be corrected and why speedy justice should not be done the parties in that behalf.

Witness the Honorable —— ——, judge of ——, this —— day of ——, A. D. 18—.

—— ——,
Judge of ——.

BILL OF REVIVOR.

[*Entitle as before.*]

To —— ——, the Judges of said Court:

Complainant herein avers and shows to this honorable court that since the beginning of this suit [*here insert event that has caused the abatement and necessity of reviving the cause, as the death of party, and set forth who are the representatives, heirs or others against whom it is sought to revive*].

Wherefore, by reason of the premises, this suit has become abated; and to revive and further proceed therewith it has become necessary to make said —— —— and —— —— parties hereto, to which end complainant prays that process by subpœna may be issued to said —— —— and —— —— requiring them to appear and show cause why said suit should not be revived against them and they be required to abide the orders and decree of the court in the premises.

BILL OF REVIEW FOR ERRORS ON FACE OF RECORD.

[*Entitle as before.*]

—— ——
—— —— } Bill of review on behalf of —— ——.
—— ——

To the Judges of said Court:

Complainant herein avers and shows that in a certain suit entitled as above, and brought in this court to the —— term, 18—, thereof, this complainant was defendant [*or,* complainant] therein, and that at the —— term, 18—, of said court, upon a hearing therein, a final decree was entered in said cause greatly to the prejudice and injury of your complainant, which said decree is entered at large upon the records of this court, and to which reference is prayed. And complainant avers and says that said decree so entered is upon the face of the record erroneous for that [*here set forth the particular matters in which error is alleged, and show how such alleged errors prejudice complainant*].

Wherefore, as said errors appear on the face of the record, and are greatly prejudicial to complainant and his rights in the premises, complainant prays that said decree may be reviewed, reversed and set aside. And to that end complainant prays process by subpœna against —— —— requiring him to appear and answer hereto and show cause, if he may, why said decree should not be reviewed, reversed and set aside, and such further orders and decrees be made as to the court may seem just.

BILL OF REVIEW ON GROUND OF NEW MATTER.

[*Entitle as before.*]

—— ——
——   } Bill of review on behalf of —— ——.
—— ——.

To the Judges of said Court:

Complainant avers and shows that in a certain suit entitled as above, and brought in this court to the —— term, 18—, thereof, this complainant was defendant [*or*, complainant] therein, and that at the —— term, 18—, of said court, upon a hearing therein, a final decree therein was entered in said cause greatly to the prejudice and injury of this complainant, which said decree is entered at large upon the records of this court and to which reference is prayed.

And this complainant avers and says that lately and since the entry of said final decree aforesaid he hath discovered that [*here set forth the new matter or the new evidence relied on as ground of review, with proper averments to show its materiality, and also show that the party was not in fault in not adducing such matter at the hearing*].

Wherefore, for said causes alleged, said decree should be reviewed, reversed and set aside; and to the end that complainant may be permitted to show and prove the matters aforesaid, complainant prays process by subpœna against —— ——, requiring him to appear hereto and due answer make, and that upon the hearing hereof the said decree may be reviewed, reversed and set aside, and such other and further orders and decree be made as may to the court seem proper.

UNITED STATES OF AMERICA, }
    District of ——. }

I, —— ——, being duly sworn, do say that I am complainant in the foregoing bill of review, that I have read the same, and that the matters and things therein set forth are true.

Subscribed and sworn to before me this —— day of ——.

—— ——.

WRIT OF NE EXEAT.

[*Entitle as before.*]

The President of the United States, To —— ——, the United States Marshal in and for District of ——:

Whereas in the above entitled cause in equity now pending in the United States circuit court in and for the —— district of ——, it has been made to appear by satisfactory proof to the said court [*or*, to the circuit justice or judge] that —— ——, defendant in said cause, is equitably indebted to the complainant, and that the said —— ——, defendant, designs quickly to depart from the United States, and thereby defeat the remedy sought by complainant and greatly to prejudice the rights of said complainant:

Therefore you are hereby ordered and commanded that without delay you cause the said —— —— to give good and sufficient bail or security in the sum of —— dollars, to be by you approved, that he will not depart beyond the limits of the United States without leave of this court first had; and in case said —— ——, defendant, fails to give bail or security as aforesaid, you are commanded to keep him in custody until the further order of court or until he gives the bail or security above required.

Witness the honorable —— ——, chief justice of the supreme court of the United States, this —— day of ——, 18—, and the seal of said circuit court in and for the —— district of ——.

—— ——, Clerk.

WRIT OF SEQUESTRATION.

[*Entitle as before.*]

The President of the United States, To —— ——:

Whereas, in the above entitled cause in equity, pending in the United States circuit court in and for the —— district of ——, it was, on the —— day of ——, ordered and decreed that —— ——, defendant, should [*here briefly state requirement of the order or decree*]. And it now appearing that the said —— ——, defendant, has wholly failed to obey and perform such order and decree, and that for such failure a writ of attachment has been hitherto duly issued from the clerk's office of this court for the attachment of the person of said defendant, but that said writ has been returned by the marshal of this district unserved for the reason that said defendant cannot be found within the jurisdiction of this court, and that for cause shown a writ of sequestration has been ordered to issue for the seizure of the estate of said —— ——, defendant, for the purpose of compelling obedience on his part to said order and decree hereinbefore mentioned:

Now, therefore, know ye that, having confidence in your prudence and fidelity, you are hereby authorized, empowered and commanded to seize and take possession of [*here describe the estate, or portion of it, to be seized, as the real and personal estate of said —— —— within ——, or certain realty or personalty*], and the rents and profits of said realty to collect and receive, and possession of said personalty to take and keep until the further order of the court in the premises.

Witness the honorable —— ——, chief justice of the supreme court of the United States, this —— day of ——, with the seal of said United States circuit court in and for —— district of ——.

RESTRAINING ORDER PENDING APPLICATION FOR INJUNCTION.

[*Entitle as before.*]

Whereas, in the above cause, a motion for the issuance of a preliminary writ of injunction has been duly filed, the hearing thereof being fixed for the —— day of ——, 18—; and it having been made to appear that there is danger of irreparable injury being caused to complainant, before the hearing of said application for the writ of injunction, unless the said defendants are, pending such hearing, restrained as herein set forth, therefore complainant's application for such restraining order is granted [*if security is required, then add*, upon his giving good security in the sum of ——, for making good to the defendants the damages and costs that may be awarded them by reason of the granting of this order]:

Now, therefore, take notice that you, —— —— and —— ——, defendants herein, your agents, servants and attorneys, and each of you, are hereby specially restrained and enjoined from [*here insert the act or acts sought to be restrained*], until the hearing upon said application for a writ of injunction and the further order of the court in the premises.

—— ——, Judge.

ORDER GRANTING PRELIMINARY INJUNCTION.

[*Entitle as before.*]

Whereas, in the above entitled cause, an application for the issuance of a preliminary writ of injunction was duly filed and set down for hearing before the court [*or*, before the Honorable G. H., a judge of said court] on the —— day of ——, 18—, at ——, notice of such application being given to —— —— and —— ——, defendants herein; and the parties now appearing by their solicitors and being heard upon such application, and it appearing that cause exists for the granting a writ of injunction, pending the final hearing of the cause, as prayed for:

It is therefore ordered that upon the complainant giving security, by bond, in the sum of ——, conditioned that [*here insert the proper conditions*], a writ of injunction issue commanding, restraining and enjoining the defendants, their agents, servants and attorneys, from [*here set forth the special matter sought to be enjoined*], until the further order of the court in the premises.

WRIT OF PRELIMINARY INJUNCTION.

[*Entitle as before*].

THE PRESIDENT OF THE UNITED STATES, To —— —— and —— ——:

Whereas, in the above entitled cause, now pending in said United States circuit court in and for the —— district of ——, upon application duly made to the court [*or if to the judge, so state, giving his name*], it was on the —— day of ——, 18—, ordered that a preliminary writ of injunction issue therein as prayed for in the bill of complaint herein filed and as directed in said order:

Now, therefore, know ye, that you, —— —— and —— ——, your agents, servants and attorneys, and each of you, are hereby strictly restrained and enjoined from [*here set forth clearly the act or acts sought to be restrained*], and you and each of you are hereby commanded that you do desist and refrain from doing or causing to be done all or any of the acts and things hereinabove recited and set forth, until the further order of the court in the premises.

Witness the Honorable —— ——, chief justice of the supreme court of the United States, this —— day of ——, and the seal of said circuit court in and for the —— district of ——.

—— ——, Clerk.

WRIT OF ASSISTANCE.

[*Entitle case as before.*]

THE PRESIDENT OF THE UNITED STATES, To —— ——, Marshal of the —— District of ——, Greeting:

Whereas in the above entitled cause it has been made to appear to the said United States circuit court in and for the —— district of ——, that under the decree of said court heretofore rendered in the above case, and the proceedings had for the enforcement thereof, the said —— ——, complainant as aforesaid [*or*, H. B., the purchaser at the foreclosure sale, *or whoever the party entitled to the writ may be*]. is now entitled to be put in possession of the following realty [*describing it*], or to have delivered up to him the following described personal property:

Now, therefore, you, as United States marshal for said —— district of ——, are hereby directed and commanded that you forthwith put the said —— —— into possession of the real estate above described [*or*, cause to be delivered to said —— —— the personal property above described], and that you cause the defendants in the above suit, their agents, servants and attorneys, to forthwith yield possession of said property in obedience to the decree heretofore entered in this case. Hereof fail not.

Witness the Honorable —— ——, chief justice of the supreme court of the United States, this —— day of ——, 18—, with the seal of said United States circuit court in and for the —— district of ——.

—— ——, Clerk.

INDEX.

In the column headed "Rules," the reference is to the Rules in Equity by their number, save when the number is preceded by the letters S. C., in which case the reference is to the Rules of the Supreme Court. All the rules thus referred to will be found on pages 143–200 of the book.

The rules of the several circuit courts of appeals will be found in volume 78 of The Federal Reporter.

In the column headed "Statutes," the reference is to the sections of the Revised Statutes, save when preceded by "Sts.," in which cases the reference is to volume and page of the Statutes at Large.

In the column headed "Page," the reference is to the top page of the Manual.

	RULES.	STATUTES.	PAGE.
ABATEMENT		955, 956; 18 Sts., 473	
ABSTRACT			
Of pleadings and evidence			85
ACCOUNTS	79		65, 66
AFFIDAVIT	80		35, 43, 105, 133
AFFIRMATION	91		35, 51
AMENDMENT		954	56
Of bills	28, 29, 45		75, 76
Of answers	60, 63, 64		57, 58, 75, 76, 77
Of decree	85		
Of process		948, 1005	
ANSWER	39, 40, 41, 42, 44, 64, 72		45, 47, 49, 50, 51, 53, 55, 57
When evidence	41		51
Form of			206
Supplemental	46		
To cross-bill	72		
APPEALS			
What cases appealable to supreme court		26 Sts., 827	99, 100
What cases appealable to circuit court of appeals		26 Sts., 828	99, 100
Appellate jurisdiction of supreme court over circuit courts of appeals		26 Sts., 828	102
By certificate	S. C. 37	26 Sts., 828	103
By *certiorari*	S. C. 37	26 Sts., 828	104
By appeal as matter of right		26 Sts., 828	105

	RULES.	STATUTES.	PAGE.
APPEALS (continued)			
Time within which, must be taken	....	1008; 26 Sts., 829	105, 107, 108, 109
How taken..................	S. C. 35	....	110, 123
By whom allowed...........	S. C. 36	999; 26 Sts., 829	113, 114
Appealable decrees..........	....	....	117, 118, 123, 125
In matter of injunctions......	....	26 Sts., 828 28 Sts., 666	120
Successive appeals..........	....	....	117
Severance among parties.....	....	....	121
Cross-appeals...............	....	....	125, 126
Who can appeal.............	....	....	122, 123
Security on appeal..........	....	1000, 1007; 26 Sts., 829	114, 115
After death of party.........	S. C. 15	....	80, 82
Petition for................	S. C. 35	....	110
Form..................	....	....	208
Transcript.................	S. C. 8	999, 1003	132
Docketing in appellate court.	S. C. 9	....	131
ASSIGNEE			
Suits by...................	....	25 Sts., 434	16
ASSIGNMENT OF ERRORS.......	S. C. 35	....	110, 112
ATTACHMENT			
Process by................	7, 8, 18, 64, 67	....	45, 57, 135, 139
To compel payment of master's compensation...............	82	....	....
AUXILIARY PROCEEDINGS.......	....	....	141
BILLS			
Suits commenced by.........	....	....	30
Introductory part............	20	....	30
Frame of..................	20, 21, 22, 23, 24, 26	....	30, 32, 33, 34, 35, 36
Where filed...............	1	....	....
Amendment of..............	28, 29, 45	....	53, 75, 76
Scandal and impertinence in.	26, 27	....	40
Form of.................	....	....	201
CHAMBERS			
Proceedings at.............	3, 4	....	7, 8
CITATION.....................	....	999	110
Form of....................	....	....	209
CIRCUIT COURT			
Court of equity............	....	629	....
Jurisdiction of............	....	629; 18 Sts., 470; 25 Sts., 433	9, 11, 12, 13, 14, 15, 16, 17, 18, 19
Under interstate commerce act	....	24 Sts., 383, 385	....
CLERK			
Duties and powers..........	....	....	6, 7
Adjourn court...............	....	672	....

	RULES.	STATUTES.	PAGE.
CLERK (continued)			
Attend on rule days.........	2		6
Enter rules, motions, or orders, etc.............	4, 6		6, 7
Enter appearance of parties......	17		46
Enter order setting down for argument.............	33, 52		54, 208
Enter pendency of suit.........	16		44
Enter report of master............	83		69
Enter return of process...........	16		
File depositions........................			69
File testimony....................	67		70
Grant motions, rules, orders, etc., as of course.........	4, 6		6, 7
Issue commissions to take testimony............	67, 70, 71		62
Issue process	7, 8, 9, 12		41, 62
Name parties to act as commissioners, when.............	67		
Publication of testimony........	69		
COMMISSIONER			
To take testimony....................	67		
Named by court, judge or clerk...	67		62
CORPORATIONS			
Citizens of states under whose laws created......			31
Mode of averment to show jurisdiction.............			32
Answer under seal.................			51
COSTS	25, 34, 35, 81	968	47, 55
CROSS-BILL			
By whom filed.....................			95
Proceedings on....................	72		96
DEATH OF PARTY			
Suggestion of.....................		955	78
Substitution of representative....	S. C. 15	955; 18 Sts., 473	78, 79, 80
DECREE			
On default........................	19		45
Form of...........................	86		86
Correction of.....................	85		
Interlocutory.....................			118
Final.............................			118
Lien.............................		25 Sts., 357	135
DEFAULT........................	18		45
DEMURRER TO BILL.........			47
Supported by certificate of counsel and affidavit of party........	31		48
General...........................			49
Form of.......................			203
Special...........................			49
Form of.......................			203
To part of bill....................	32, 36, 37		49
Form of......................			204

	RULES.	STATUTES.	PAGE.
DEMURRER TO BILL (continued)			
Set down for argument............	33	....	54
Form for....................	....	....	208
Costs on.....................	34, 35	....	55
DEPOSITIONS			
See TESTIMONY.			
ENTRY			
Final..........................	....	750	142
EQUITY			
Jurisdiction of court of.........	....	913	9, 11, 12, 13, 14, 16, 18
Suits in, not sustainable if complete remedy at law..............	....	723	10, 11
EVIDENCE......	....	862	....
Time for taking.................	69	....	60
Modes of taking.................	67, 68, 70	....	60, 61, 62, 63, 64, 65
See TESTIMONY; WITNESSES.			
EXAMINER.	67	....	61
By whom named.................	67	....	61
EXCEPTIONS			
To bills.......................	26, 27	....	46
Form of, for scandal or impertinence.............	....	....	207
To answers....................	27	....	56
To answers for insufficiency......	....	....	56
Form of.......................	....	....	207
FORECLOSURE			
Decree for balance	92	....	86
GUARDIAN			
Suit by.......................	87	....	39
HEARING			
On bill and answer	41	....	60
On exceptions.................	63	....	69
On exceptions for defect of parties	52, 53	....	52
On issue joined and evidence.....	....	....	60
IMPERTINENCE			
In bills	26, 27	....	46
In answer.....................	27	....	56
INFANTS			
Suit by.......................	87	....	39
Suit against...................	87	....	34, 39
Appeal by; time allowed	....	1008	107
INJUNCTION.................	....	719	....
By whom grantable	....	719	93
Proceedings for................	....	....	34, 93
Form of......................	....	....	214

	RULES.	STATUTES.	PAGE.
INSANE			
Suit by	87		39
Suit against	87		34
Appeal by; time allowed		1008	107
INTERLOCUTORY			
Orders grantable by clerk	5		6, 7
Grantable by court or judge	6		7
Not appealable			117
INTERROGATORIES			
In bill	40, 41, 42, 43, 44		35
Final, in depositions	71		63
INTERVENTION			
Right of			97
Petition of			97
JURISDICTION			
Of circuit courts, based on special statutes and several judiciary acts			11, 12, 13
In equity, derived from English rules, statutes of United States and statutes of states			9
Adequate remedy at law defeats		723	10, 11
MANDATE	S. C. 39		134
MARSHAL			
General duties and powers		787, 788	
Adjournment of court		671, 672	
Service of process by	15		41, 42
Return of process by	16		44
MASTER			
Appointment of	82		60, 65
Compensation of	82		
Proceedings before	73, 74, 75, 77, 79, 80, 81		66, 67, 68, 69
Report of	75, 76		68
Exceptions to report of	83, 84		69
MISJOINDER			
Ground for demurrer to bill			48
MOTIONS			
Entry of	1, 2, 4		8
Grantable of course	5		6, 7
Upon order or notice	3, 6		7, 8
NE EXEAT			
Writ of		717	42
Prayer for	23		34, 35
Form of			212
NEXT FRIEND			
Suit by	87		39

	RULES.	STATUTES.	PAGE.
NON-JOINDER			
Ground for demurrer to bill	47, 48, 49		48
Exceptions to bill for	52		52
NOTICE			
When entry in order book is	4		8
To solicitors, when sufficient	4		8
ORDERS			
Entry in book by clerk	4		8
Grantable by clerk	5		6
Grantable by court or judge	1, 3, 4, 6		7
Deemed abandoned	27, 30, 63		47, 57
PARTIES			
All interested should be made	47		38
Indispensable, being absent, no decree			39
If parties cannot be brought in, decree may be granted if their rights may be saved	47		27, 38
Nominal	54		16
Numerous	48		38
Heirs	50		40
Joint debtors	51		39
Trustees	49		
Defect of, how availed of			48, 50, 52
PETITION			
Of intervention			97
For rehearing	88		86
PLACE OF SUIT			
See VENUE.			
PLEA			
Time of filing	32		47
Certificate of counsel	31		48
Form of			204
Affidavit of defendant	31		48
Form of			205
To part or whole of bill	32, 36, 37		50
Form of			205
Argument on	33		51
Issue on	33		51
Admission of	38		
Nature of			50
Matter of			50
Abatement should be by	39		50
In bar			50
PLEADING			
Modes and forms prescribed by supreme court		913, 917	6
PRACTICE IN EQUITY			
To conform to established usage, the statutes and rules of supreme and circuit courts	89, 90	913, 917, 918	6

	RULES.	STATUTES.	PAGE.
PRAYER			
For mesne process........	23		34
Form of......			201, 202
For relief...............	21		34
Form of......			201
PRÆCIPE			
For process..............			41
Form of......			202
PROCESS			
Mesne			
Subpœna for defendant.......	7		41
Subpœna for witnesses........	78		72, 73
Attachment...................	7		45
Injunction...................	55		93
Restraining order............		718	94
Final			
Attachment...................	8		135
Assistance...................	7, 9		139
Execution....................	8		138
Injunction...................		4921	
Restitution..................			139
Sequestration................	7		140
REFERENCE			
Of exceptions............	26, 27		47, 56
Of issues................	73, 74		60, 65
REHEARING			
Applied for by petition..	88		86
Time of filing...........	88		87
REPLICATION			
General only.............	45		58
When filed...............	66		58
Form of..................			207
RESTRAINING ORDER		718	94
Form of..................			213
REVIEW			
Bill of, when grantable..			87, 88
Form of..................			210, 211
REVIVOR			
Bill of..................	56, 57		78
On suggestion of death...	S. C. 15		79
Form of bill of....			209
RULE DAY.............................	2		6, 7
RULES IN EQUITY......................			6, 143
RULES OF SUPREME COURT...............			177
SALES BY MASTER......................			136
SCANDAL			
In bill or answer........	25, 27		46, 56

	RULES.	STATUTES.	PAGE.
SECURITY ON APPEAL............	S. C. 29	1000, 1007, 1012	114, 115
SEQUESTRATION			
Writ of............................	7	....	140
Form of............................	....	....	212
SERVICE OF PROCESS			
By whom made..................	15	....	41
How made.......................	13	....	41
SETTING DOWN FOR ARGUMENT			
Demurrer........................	33	....	54
Form of........................	....	....	208
Plea.............................	33	....	54
Form of........................	....	....	208
Answer suggesting defect of parties...................	52	....	52
Form of........................	....	....	208
STATUTORY PROVISIONS AFFECTING CIRCUIT COURT AND PRACTICE			
Abatement	....	955, 956; 18 Sts., 473	....
Adjournment of court...........	....	672	....
Amendment of process and pleadings	....	918, 954, 1005	....
Appeal	....	692, 699, 1008, 1012	....
To supreme court..............	....	26 Sts., 827	....
To circuit court of appeals.....	....	26 Sts., 828	....
To supreme from circuit court of appeals......................	....	26 Sts., 828	....
By infant, insane or prisoner..	....	1008	....
On death of party.............	....	955, 956	....
Assignee			
Suit by.........................	....	25 Sts., 433	....
Circuit court			
Creation and organization.....	....	605–628	....
Jurisdiction.			
Under judiciary acts...........	....	Title XIII, R. S.; 18 Sts., 470; 25 Sts., 433	....
Under special acts			
Revenue from imports, tonnage or internal taxes.......	....	692	....
Patents.....................	....	692; 29 Sts., 692, 695	....
Copyrights..................	....	957; 28 Sts., 965; 29 Sts., 483–691	....
Trade-marks................	....	21 Sts., 502	....
National bank acts...........	....	1012; 25 Sts., 436	....
Interstate commerce.........	....	24 Sts., 380; 25 Sts., 855	....
Trusts......................	....	26 Sts., 209	....
Tariff duties...............	....	26 Sts., 131	....
Condemnation of land for public use......................	....	25 Sts., 357	....
Unlawful occupancy of public lands.......................	....	23 Sts., 321	....

INDEX.

	RULES.	STATUTES.	PAGE.
STATUTORY PROVISIONS AFFECTING CIRCUIT COURT AND PRACTICE (continued)			
Under special acts (continued)			
Immigration and alien contract labor..........	....	26 Sts., 1084	....
Suits against the United States	....	24 Sts., 505	....
Death of party....................	....	955	....
Decree, lien of	....	18 Sts., 473; 25 Sts., 357	....
Evidence			
Mode of proof................	....	862	....
Witness, who competent......	....	858	....
Privileged...................	....	859, 860	....
Injunction			
When and by whom grantable.	....	719	....
Continuance of...............	....	719	....
Jurisdiction			
See CIRCUIT COURT.			
National banks			
Jurisdiction limited...........	....	25 Sts., 436	....
Pleading......................	....	913, 917	....
Practice.......................	....	913, 918	....
Process, form of	....	911, 912, 918	....
By whom served............	....	922	....
Amendment of................	....	948	....
Receivers			
Jurisdiction	....	25 Sts., 436	....
Restraining order on application for injunction	....	718	....
Security on appeal............	....	1000, 1007, 1012	....
Subpœna for witnesses	....	868	....
Duces tecum	....	869	....
Supersedeas	....	1000, 1007, 1012	....
Witnesses			
Who competent..............	....	858	....
Privilege	....	859, 860	....
Fees of	....	848	....
Testimony of, taken *de bene*..	....	863, 864, 865	....
On *dedimus*.................	....	866	....
Under state statute...........	....	27 Sts., 7	....
Distance may be required to travel...	....	876, 870	....
Writs			
Power to issue	....	716	....
Of injunction.................	....	719	....
Of *ne exeat*.................	....	717	....
STOCKHOLDER			
Bill by	94	....	36
SUBPŒNA			
Issued by clerk	12	....	41
Not until bill filed.	12	....	41
Returnable......................	12	....	41
Service of, how made............	13	....	41
By whom served........	15	....	41
Alias issued....................	14	....	42

	RULES.	STATUTES.	PAGE.
SUBPŒNA FOR WITNESSES			
Issued by clerk	78	868	72
Duces tecum		869	73
SUPPLEMENTAL BILL	57		77
SUPERSEDEAS		1000, 1007, 1012	
Security and condition of bond	S. C. 29		114, 116
In case of injunction	93	28 Sts., 666	115, 116
TESTIMONY			60
Time for taking	69		60
How taken	67, 68		60, 61, 62, 63, 64, 65
Of aged; infirm			64
About to leave			64
Single witness	70		64
De bene esse		863, 864, 865	63
Dedimus		866	64
According to state statutes		27 Sts., 7	64
Abstract on hearing			85
Publication of	69		
TRANSCRIPT			
On appeal, contents of	S. C. 8	698	132
Filing	S. C. 9		131
UNITED STATES CIRCUIT COURTS		629; 18 Sts., 470: 25 Sts., 433	
VENUE		742	20
Local actions		18 Sts., 470 25 Sts., 433	22
Patents		29 Sts., 695	24
Transitory		25 Sts., 433	23, 24, 25, 26
Waiver of objection to venue			25
VERIFICATION OF ANSWER			
Before whom	59		51
WRIT			
Attachment	7, 8		
Assistance	7-9		215
Execution	8		
Injunction	55	719	214
Sequestration	7		212
Restitution			

www.ingramcontent.com/pod-product-compliance
Lightning Source LLC
Chambersburg PA
CBHW021833230426
43669CB00008B/953